D1647752

COUNT THESE HINTS INSTEAD OF SHEEP!

- Is there a medical cause for your insomnia? (See Rule #1.)
- Do you go to bed at different times every night? (See Rule #6.)
- Do you exercise regularly? (See Rule #25.)
- Do you eat carbohydrates before going to bed? (See Rule #32.)
- Are you getting enough calcium, magnesium, copper, and iron? (See Rule #39.)
- Do you get enough sunlight? (See Rule #51.)

With 67 tips in all,
you can count on getting good sleep!

By Charles B. Inlander and Cynthia K. Moran
Published by Ballantine Books:

77 WAYS TO BEAT COLDS AND FLU
67 WAYS TO GOOD SLEEP

67 WAYS TO GOOD SLEEP

**Charles B. Inlander
and Cynthia K. Moran**

FAWCETT CREST • NEW YORK

A Fawcett Crest Book
Published by Ballantine Books
Copyright © 1995 by People's Medical Society

http://www.randomhouse.com

Library of Congress Catalog Card Number: 95-90827

ISBN 0-449-22473-2

A note to the reader: The ideas, procedures, and suggestions contained in this book are not intended as a substitute for consulting with your practitioner. All matters regarding your health require medical supervision.

This edition published by arrangement with Walker and Company.

Manufactured in the United States of America

First Ballantine Books Edition: April 1996

10 9 8 7 6 5 4 3 2 1

Contents

**Appendix C: Benzodiazepines Used for
               Sleep-Disorder Treatment**........107

Introduction

Good night!

These two calming and soothing words can be the wrap-up to a wonderful day or the welcome to a night of restful slumber. But for tens of millions of Americans, these simple words can be the harbinger of a night of restlessness and sleeplessness, followed by a day of fatigue and anguish.

No problem affects more Americans, more often, than insomnia and other related sleep disorders. Poor sleep saps energy, increases anxiety, and costs up to $64 billion annually in on-the-job accidents and lost productivity.

That's the bad news.

Here's the good news. Insomnia and other sleep disorders can be prevented and treated. In 67 WAYS TO GOOD SLEEP, we show you how to get a good night's sleep in easy-to-read, understandable tips.

In developing this book, Cynthia Moran and I recognized that sleep is highly individualized. We also knew that sleep needs and patterns change over a person's lifetime. All that was taken into consideration as we wrote and edited this book. Whether you are 7 or 70 and are the picture of health or suffer from several physical ailments, 67 WAYS TO GOOD SLEEP has help for you.

Charles B. Inlander, President
People's Medical Society

67 WAYS
TO GOOD SLEEP

1
•
Understanding Sleep

Just a century ago, sleep was considered little more than a nightly vegetative state, a time when daily pursuits were stilled for 8 to 10 hours. The brain temporarily ceased to function, and the body disengaged, entering into total, quiet rest. Insomnia—the inability to fall or stay asleep—was an inexplicable curiosity: It afflicted many, struck at random, and had, went the thinking, no precise cause or cure. Dreams, nightmares, and sleepwalking were more the province of poets and playwrights than of scientists or medical experts.

In the 1930s, with the first use of electroencephalograms (EEGs) to study human brain waves, the doors to understanding sleep began to creak open. But not until 1953, when scientists verified the phenomenon of rapid eye movement (REM) during sleep, did the field of sleep science become established. The discovery of the existence of REM offered first proof that in sleep the body is not at total rest.

Sleep, it turns out, is a highly complex activity. Today we are still learning about sleep, but research has established certain facts:

• **Too little sleep can make us sick.** A recent study, at the University of California at San Diego, found that some immune-system activities decrease as much as 30 percent after nights when people miss three or more hours of sleep.

• **"Sleeping on it" isn't an empty expression.** Sleeping allows the brain to consolidate the day's learning into the memory. Thus, what is new and confusing today may be better understood tomorrow, after a good night's sleep.

• **Most people with sleep problems do not seek professional help, and most physicians cannot spot a sleep problem without being prompted.**

In 1988 Congress created the National Commission on Sleep Disorders and Research, whose final report, published in early 1993, was eye-opening. The Commission found that:

• One in three Americans—36 percent—doesn't get enough sleep.

• At least 40 million Americans suffer chronic sleep disorders, and 20 to 30 million more suffer intermittent insomnia serious enough to put themselves (and others) at risk of injury or illness.

• Serious sleep deprivation directly cost the U.S. economy $15.83 billion in 1990, a figure that outstripped the costs of AIDS and cigarette damage for the same year.

• Some 40,000 persons a year die and another 250,000 are injured after falling asleep at the wheel, according to the Highway Safety Commission. The Department of Transportation estimates that 200,000 highway accidents a year are sleep related.

• Four percent of American adults reported using sleep medications in 1990, while another 3 percent said they bought over-the-counter sleep aids.

• There are 17 distinct sleep disorders identified by the Commission report. Ninety-five percent of them go undiagnosed and therefore untreated.

What's Keeping Us Awake?

We live at a frenzied pace, a pace unheard of just a few decades ago. "Today cultural and economic forces combine to create a 24-hour society in which millions of Americans obtain insufficient sleep as a result of workplace and lifestyle determinants," reported the Commission. From shopping at all-night supermarkets to working in shift factories offering double overtime, many Americans are severely deprived of adequate sleep and, therefore, are sleepy during the day.

With the advent of electric service throughout our country, we got the opportunity to live a longer day than our ancestors did. With modern society's complexities and schedules, Americans in the 1990s sleep about 20 percent less than their counterparts in the 1890s. Part of this loss of sleep can be attributed to the fact that, compared with 100 years ago, we work and commute 158 more hours a year! That's the equivalent of slightly more than an additional month of work days.

The dangers of sleep deprivation can be enormous. The Exxon *Valdez* grounding, the Chernobyl nuclear leak, the Bhopal pesticide explosion, and the loss of the spaceship *Challenger* all had elements of sleep deprivation noted in their official reports of cause.

Awakening Our Knowledge

Surveys reveal widespread ignorance about sleep and how to find help for solving sleep problems. Stanford University sleep researchers believe that Americans don't seek proper help because "they devalue sleep," rushing to cram increasingly more activities into already full days, in which sleep becomes the only expendable activity.

Plus, there is the fear of stigmatization. For some

individuals, seeking professional help for a sleep disorder is the equivalent of publicly announcing a serious mental disorder. Consequently, these people not only fail to receive help with their problems, but also remain relatively uneducated about causes and treatments.

Finally, the medical profession itself is relatively uneducated about the subject—so much so that in 1993 Stanford University researchers urged the American Medical Association to push for "better medical education and training in the diagnosis and management of sleep disorders."

So let's get educated. If you're affected by sleep loss and you're determined to attack your problem, here's a crash course on the A-B-Zs of sleep.

What Is Sleep?

Sleep is a natural period within every 24 hours when the body repairs itself, tests its systems, consolidates memory, purges itself of cellular waste, and stockpiles energy for the day ahead. On average, humans spend about a third of their lives asleep, or about 205,000 hours in a 70-year lifetime.

Dianne Hales, author of *How to Sleep Like a Baby**explains that when we sleep, "we are not motionless like a car in a garage. [Sleep] is an altered

*New York: Ballantine Books, 1987.

form of consciousness, when muscles tense and relax, our pulse, like our temperature and blood pressure, rises and falls, the brain works, and chemicals course through the bloodstream."

Good sleep is harder to define, but we know it when we see it. Deepak Chopra, M.D., describes good quality sleep in his book, *Restful Sleep: The Complete Mind/Body Program for Overcoming Insomnia,** as "sleep that seems to happen by itself. . . . You rarely wake up in the middle of the night from good sleep, but if you do, you get back to sleep quickly without worrying about it. . . . You wake up naturally in the morning. You're neither sluggish and groggy nor anxious and hyperalert. [Good sleep] provides you with a sense of vitality that lasts throughout the day. You don't feel you've been deprived of rest during the preceding night, and you don't feel anxious about what's going to happen the next time you try to fall asleep."

Sleep can be broken down into two major classes or periods, REM (rapid eye movement) and NREM (non–rapid eye movement), which alternate in 90-minute cycles throughout a typical seven-to-eight-hour night.

REM sleep is the shallower sleep cycle associated with dreaming, when body temperature and blood pressure rise, breathing is shallower and faster, and brain function is as active as it is in a wakeful person.

*New York: Harmony Books, 1994.

In NREM sleep, brain function is much less active, only infrequent (and forgotten) dreaming is thought to occur, and the deep, restorative sleep necessary to our physical well-being takes place.

The chart on pages 12 and 13 details the stages of sleep.

Internal Clocks

The human body is governed by two complex, clock-like systems: one to promote sleep (the circadian clock), the other to promote arousal (the homeostatic clock). Together they govern our daily sleep-wake cycle.

Technically, the circadian clock is known as circadian rhythm—from the Latin *circa* meaning "around" and *dian* meaning "day." Circadian rhythm refers to the human body's rhythm patterns of "about a day," which for most adults is a 25-hour cycle. But we have forced it into a 24-hour rhythm to coincide with Earth's daily revolutions into daylight and dark, thus synchronizing us with the rest of the world.

A key function of the circadian rhythm is to control body temperature, the single strongest cue in the sleep-wake cycle. When our temperature is highest, we are most alert and function the best. When it is lowest, we are drowsy. The average adult experiences two temperature peaks—one in midmorning, the other in midevening.

The second internal timekeeping mechanism is the homeostatic clock, with a cycle of 28 hours. Neuroendocrinologists at Brigham and Women's Hospital in Boston, experts on the interaction of the body's two clocks, theorize that the homeostatic clock prompts us to go to sleep in the late evening and, without circadian coordination, would cause us to awake in only three to four hours. But the circadian clock kicks in late at night to allow us to sleep longer.

With two internal clocks always (except in cases of sleep disorders) running on different schedules, synchronization becomes critical for normal sleep. Sleep scientists explain that we coordinate these schedules daily by imposing recurring time cues called *zeitgebers*, German for *time-givers*. By resetting these two internal clocks daily, we force them into a regular, 24-hour rhythm compatible with our external world schedule. Nothing fancy, zeitgebers range from alarm clocks to regular, self-imposed wakeup and bedtimes, and presleep rituals. At various stages of our lives, our normal circadian rhythms change, running longer or shorter than our self-imposed 24-hour patterns. At these times, unless we're vigilant, we start running "out of sync" with the rest of the world.

Older sleepers, for example, run on a shorter rhythm (faster clock) than 24 hours, a principal reason many older sleepers awake as early as 3 a.m., primed to arise for the day. For these sleepers, the most critical zeitgeber is a regular, late-evening bedtime that is not permitted to slide back to an earlier time, even if the person feels tired at 8 p.m.

Brainpower

Manufactured by the nervous system, hormonelike chemicals called neurotransmitters conduct nerve signals among the brain cells. Increasingly, sleep research is establishing the central role played by the manufacture, release, and use of these key brain chemicals in the sleep-wake cycle. Six neurotransmitters in particular—cortisol, melatonin, serotonin, epinephrine, norepinephrine, and dopamine—are worth mentioning:

• **Cortisol** (also called hydrocortisone) supply in the body peaks at 6 a.m. and runs down about midnight. When it runs into short supply at day's end (as it is naturally supposed to), the action cues body temperature to fall and the mind to wind down, become less alert, and prepare for sleep. Drowsiness results.

• **Melatonin** induces sleep by helping to control circadian (light-dark) rhythm. The brain's secretions of melatonin are stimulated by darkness.

• **Serotonin** is believed to be the key neurotransmitter of sleep biology, since it appears to control states of consciousness as well as mood and sensitivity to pain. Like cortisol, it is thought to affect body temperature changes; therefore, it has bearing on the sleep-wake cycle. Scientists believe serotonin accrues in the body during deep sleep.

• **Epinephrine** (adrenaline), **norepinephrine** (noradrenaline), and **dopamine** are the neurotransmitters most active during periods of stress or emergency. They enliven the brain and make you alert, more attentive, motivated, and mentally energetic.

How Much Sleep Do You Need?

As with hair color and height, the amount of sleep a person needs differs by individual physiology, by age, and, at times, even by gender. Adult sleep needs range from 5 to 10 hours a night, with the average adult needing between 7 and 8 hours. Statistics show that only 1 person in 1,000 can get by on fewer than 4½ hours of sleep.

A look at sleep needs by age-group versus what each group is actually getting, according to the National Commission survey released in 1993, shows:

• Babies need and receive 18 hours per day.

• Young to preteenage children need and generally receive 10 to 12 hours (8 after they stop napping).

• Teens need up to 10 hours and average 6.

• Adults need an average of 7 to 9 hours and get fewer than 7.

• The elderly need about 8 hours and get 5 to 7 (some a bit more with naps).

But these figures are simply averages. They may not apply exactly to you. So here's a simple home test suggested by health writer Joan Barbato in an August 28, 1994, *Star-Ledger* article: "You are probably not getting enough sleep if you frequently: are drowsy when driving; get into accidents; are irritable; have impaired memory; have difficulty making decisions; wake up tired; feel your productivity diminish; sleep longer and feel better when the weekend comes."

Loss of sleep accumulates, so sleep debt, or deficit, is the cumulative total of sleep hours you are behind. Stanford University's sleep-research pioneer William C. Dement, M.D., explains in a November 23, 1994, *Family Circle* article: "Until you sleep, that debt remains unsatisfied in the same way that you're thirsty until you drink." In other words, you can resist, but eventually the debt will overwhelm you.

The good news? A reasonably healthy human is remarkably resilient and is able to reduce or repay a sleep debt with just a little concerted effort. "Even if the person's missed *all* sleep for 10 days," notes Mayo Clinic sleep expert Peter Hauri, Ph.D., in *No More Sleepless Nights*,* "a sleep of 14 to 18 hours a

*New York: John Wiley & Sons, 1990.

A Sleep Cycle That's Repeated Four to Six Times Nightly

PHASE	STAGE	DURATION	OBSERVATIONS
NREM Sleep (Non–Rapid Eye Movement Sleep, orthodox sleep) 80% of entire night's sleep in adults; in early cycles, most time spent in NREM. Thought to restore, rejuvenate, revitalize physical functions of body.	Zero (Wakefulness, presleep stage)	Few minutes to 30+ minutes; only experienced at start of sleep.	Akin to meditative state; conscious of surroundings.
	Stage 1 (Drowsiness, shallow or light sleep)	5–10% of entire night's sleep in adults. First cycle: 30 seconds–7 minutes.	Transitional stage; no recovery or restorative value; alert if aroused; may feel as though still awake; floating, falling feelings; muscle jerks.
	Stage 2 (Deeper stage, true sleep)	10–20% of entire night's sleep in adults. First cycle: 10–25 minutes.	Beginning to drift into sound sleep; fragmented thoughts, images pass through mind; can't see, even if eyes open; unaware of surroundings; relatively alert awakening from this stage.
	Stage 3 (Delta or slow-wave sleep; often described in combination with Stage 4)	50% of entire night's sleep in adults (disappears in 5th+ cycles); First cycle: 3–5 minutes.	Deep, restful, restorative sleep; skeletal muscle protein synthesis; immune function maintenance; arousal difficult. Stage 3 deprivation results in next-day feelings of fatigue, lethargy, apathy, depression; Stage 3 sleep decreases with age.

PHASE	STAGE	DURATION	OBSERVATIONS
NREM Sleep (continued)	**Stage 4** (Delta or slow-wave sleep; deepest sleep; restorative sleep)	With Stage 3, up to 50% of entire night's sleep in adults, lessens with age. **First cycle:** 20–40 minutes; stops after first third of night when NREM reaches only Stage 3.	Deepest, most restorative phase; arousal most difficult. Mental recovery; blood directed to brain. Growth hormones, protein synthesis, immune function maintenance. Helped by exercise; hurt by psychoactive drugs, alcohol. Stage lessens for men in 30s; for women, in 50s. If sleep deprived, catch-up time needed here and in REM.
REM Sleep (*Rapid Eye Movement Sleep, paradoxical sleep, dreaming sleep*) Up to 25% of entire night's sleep in adults, mostly occurring in last third of sleep. Thought to consolidate, restore memory functions; vital also to mental health.		20–25% of entire night's sleep in adults, diminishes with age. **First REM period:** 5–10 minutes, occurring 90–100 minutes into sleep cycle; by 4th–5th cycles, lasts up to an hour.	REM dreams can have elaborate story lines, often recalled upon awakening. REM sleep may be needed to sort through short-term memory storage, deleting unnecessary data, laying down important information in long-term memory. Psychoactive drugs, including alcohol, hinder REM sleep. Continued loss of REM sleep creates anxiety, emotional difficulties until sleep debt erased. Insomniacs tend to spend less time in REM sleep than in other stages.

day for three days followed by returning to a normal schedule will eliminate the debt." The typical formula, according to experts, is: One hour of sleep can repay two lost hours of sleep.

Now that you have a working knowledge of sleep and the complex mechanisms behind it, let's look at ways to maximize good sleep.

2
•

Tips on How to
Get Better Sleep

If there is a silver lining in the cloud over American sleeplessness, it is that a majority of us—some 60 to 70 percent—have the kinds of insomnia that respond well to self-help. We can use stress reduction, improved nutrition and sleep habits, and modified lifestyle choices to help us sleep better.

In this chapter we suggest ways you can assess your sleep-wake patterns. Once you've gathered specific data on your sleep problem, you then can select the tips that make the most sense for your circumstances. Try pertinent tips for at least two weeks (the minimum time, experts say, for your sleep cycle to reflect changes). If you do not notice an improvement in your sleep, you may then want to seek additional help, which we detail for you in Chapter 3.

At the very outset, here is what you should do to get better sleep:

✔ **1** *Rule out medical causes of insomnia.*

Before doing anything else, determine whether your problem is a case of insomnia (an inability to fall asleep or stay asleep or sleep well) or a sign of a more serious medical and/or psychological condition. Scores of medical conditions—intestinal malabsorption problems, heart disease, diabetes, anemia, yeast infections and chronic sinus infections, just to name a few—include insomnia as a secondary effect. The fact is that almost every medical condition can create a concurrent sleep problem.

Over 120 forms of sleep disorders have been identified, and as more brain and cellular-biology research results are published, more are being added to the list. They are grouped to indicate whether the condition originates inside the body (intrinsic), in the external environment (extrinsic and circadian), or in abnormal sleep-associated behavior (parasomnia). (See Appendix A for short symptomatic descriptions of the most common adult sleep disorders.)

So, before you spend a lot of time trying to improve your sleep with self-help tips, have a full medical exam to rule out medical causes. David S. Bell, M.D., author of *Chronic Fatigue,** recommends your exam include at least the following: the American Cancer Society's full cancer-screening tests; a com-

*Emmaus, Pa.: Rodale Press, 1993.

plete blood count (CBC) to rule out anemia or chronic infection; a sedimentation rate test to screen for a variety of medical abnormalities; tests of routine chemistries to rule out problems arising from thyroid conditions or arthritis; and a chest x-ray.

By heightening your self-awareness and improving sleep habits as the tips suggest, you could conceivably diminish or arrest a case of transient (short-term) insomnia or one of the milder extrinsic or circadian disorders. A number of sleep disorders have multiple causes, however, some of which may have deep-seated, complex roots that must be uncovered with the help of a doctor or sleep lab before they can be eliminated. Others, such as those related to chronic pain or a lingering medical condition, will not be cured by following our tips, but you may notice beneficial effects that improve your sleep. Finally, if you have a sleep disorder that can be conquered only with medical and/or pharmacological intervention, our tips can help you focus on your symptoms and gather information that your doctor or sleep lab will find pertinent to your treatment.

✔ **2 Find out if any medications you're taking are eye-openers.**

This is a logical, early step in trying to uncover the reason for your sleeplessness, for the simple reason that dozens of widely used medications taken for various medical conditions contain ingredients that preclude sleep. Drugs that can keep you up at night include those containing caffeine (including some over-the-counter painkillers—for example Excedrin and Anacin—as well as prescription-only concoctions); diet aids that contain amphetamines; alertness pills, such as NoDoz and Vivarin; some allergy medications, especially any containing ACTH, a stimulant hormone; nasal decongestants, such as Sudafed and Sinutab; blood-pressure medications; many asthma drugs; steroid preparations; thyroid hormones; various beta blockers (taken for heart disease and high blood pressure); some antidepressants; and some anti-metabolites used in cancer treatments. Check package inserts or ask your pharmacist or doctor to identify any caffeine-containing medications you may be taking.

If it's an over-the-counter medication you're using, try changing the times you take it or reducing the dosage level. Even with a prescription medication, it's possible that your doctor can change either the dosage or the hour of day you take it or switch you to a related drug that doesn't affect sleep, suggests sleep author James Perl, Ph.D., in the February/March 1994 issue of *Remedy*.

✔ 3 Review your genetic sleep blueprint.

A number of sleep disorders—sleepwalking, chronic insomnia, and narcolepsy among them—are often hereditary. So if you have a sleep-related problem, chances are good that an immediate family member has or had a similar problem. (It's also possible, of course, that you're the first.) Interview family members, telling them about your problem and asking if they have ever experienced similar difficulties. You may discover that there is a pattern of sleeplessness in your family, a revelation that can help you in your own quest for good sleep.

✔ **4** *Keep a written sleep log for at least one week, preferably two.*

You cannot begin to resolve a sleep problem until you know in detail your own sleep habits. A discipline of sorts, keeping a sleep log is hardest the first several days, because it means conditioning yourself to pause at least twice a day—just after awaking and prior to bedtime—to recall and commit to paper your activities and feelings. Make entries in your log within 30 minutes of awaking in the morning: at night, record your evening's data within 30 minutes of bedtime.

Your log should cover such topics as when you went to bed, how long it took you to get to sleep, how many times you recall waking during the night, what mood you were in just before bedtime, what personal interactions you had in the evening, what you ate for dinner and snacks, and whether you exercised, drank alcohol or caffeine, or had a cigarette within three hours of bedtime.

Sleep logs help you learn things about yourself that you may not have considered before. One confirmed insomniac was surprised to learn, after keeping a log for two weeks, that the three nights she had the worst sleep were all preceded by upsetting phone calls from her elderly mother. She had never previously made the connection before to the anxiety that relationship created in her life and the effects it had on her sleep.

✔ **5** Quiz *yourself.*

Remember, losing sleep can stem from any one of a variety of causes or a combination of them. Sleep-loss diagnosticians often begin evaluating patients by asking them to complete short, self-administered quizzes. Questions are, for example: Do you lie awake for half an hour or more before falling asleep? Do you feel you have to cram a full day into every hour to get anything done? Does your heart pound or beat irregularly during the night? Do you suddenly wake up gasping for breath during the night? Have you fallen asleep while driving? Do you have vivid nightmares soon after falling asleep? Have you been told you kick at night? Do you experience aching or "crawling" sensations in your legs at night?

More detailed than a sleep log about your overall lifestyle, these questionnaires seek to illuminate possible trouble spots—anxiety level and mental state, nutrition patterns, exercise and fitness levels, and other habits—that may be responsible for your poor sleep.

Now that you've assembled your sleep history and symptoms, here are tips for getting better sleep on your own.

Sleep Habits

✔ **6** *Establish a regular bedtime and rising time, and stick to them.*

Sleep experts agree that such a regimen is the most important sleep cue of all. A regular bedtime and rising time can help you stabilize your internal clocks. Select a bedtime that's good and natural for you. A clue that you're getting to bed at a good hour is a lack of daytime sleepiness. Don't change your bedtime and rising time on weekends. Reprogramming your sleep rhythms for two days doesn't do much to help you erase sleep debt, and it throws your sleep-wake cycles off in time for a good case of Sunday night insomnia.

✔ **7** *Avoid physical and mental stimulation just before sleep.*

But don't avoid sex (more about that below). Physical exertion too close to bedtime energizes your body's systems by stimulating the release of adrenaline. (As we detail later, the best sleep-inducing exercise is an aerobic session done five to six hours before bedtime.) Mental stimulation includes any activity that taxes your mind or gets your thoughts racing, such as watching an action-packed TV show. Similarly, planning tomorrow's schedule, doing office reading, or reading a chapter from a convoluted murder mystery moments before turning out the light does not give you adequate time to disengage from mental activity before trying to sleep.

✔ 8 Try sex.

Research shows that sexual stimulation releases endorphins, hormones that make you mellow and relaxed. Making love just before you and your partner sleep can be a true sleep inducer, but it works only if you gain satisfaction from it. Bernard Dryer, M.D., author of *Inside Insomnia*,* suggests that if sex is too mechanistic—used only as a tool to induce sleep—it is likely to be more upsetting than helpful.

✔ 9 Keep the bedroom for sleeping and sex only.

If you use your bedroom as a place to eat, watch TV, read, talk on the phone, fight, or discuss weighty matters with your partner, break that habit to get bet-

*New York: Villard Books, 1986.

ter sleep. Sleep therapists insist that if our minds associate any other functions—besides sleep and sex—with the bedroom, we're asking for sleep problems.

✔ 10 Develop sleep rituals.

We train children to have sleep rituals and cue them by saying, "It's time to get ready for bed." But as adults most of us forget to continue the process in our own lives. Sleep rituals run the gamut, from taking the garbage out or a pet for a last walk (as long as the exercise isn't too strenuous), to watching a certain news program or weather forecast while sitting in a favorite chair, to taking a shower, brushing the teeth, donning pajamas, tucking in the kids one last time, saying prayers, or reading a book (but not a murder mystery).

✔ 11 Determine how many hours you should be sleeping.

Sleep research shows that we develop a natural sleep length early in life and seldom deviate from it other than during such periods as early childhood, adolescence, and old age, when everyone's sleep needs change proportionately. To determine your ideal length of sleep, factor in these considerations: (1) how many hours you slept on average as a child; (2) how many hours you slept each night on average before your insomnia began; (3) after how many hours' sleep you awake naturally (when you have not been overtired) without an alarm set; and (4) how many hours you must sleep so as not to experience daytime sleepiness.

If your answers are fairly consistent, you have a reasonably accurate indicator of your sleep needs. If answers vary, start with seven hours and see how that works. If, after a week of seven-hour nights, you consistently wake up too early, try shortening your night in 15-minute intervals (a week at a time) until you're sleeping better. If, on the other hand, your seven-hour night leaves you feeling daytime sleepiness, continue going to bed 15 minutes earlier until you get to a comfortable sleep length.

✔ 12 Don't go to bed too early.

Partner pressure, boredom, transient stress, or depression can propel you into a habit of going to bed before you should. Older people often go to bed too early which only adds to their problem of fragmented sleep; consequently, their overall sleep is shallower. The fact is, if you have determined that your normal sleep profile is 8 hours, sleeping 10 only spreads out the 8 and results in fragmented and less satisfying sleep. Further, since your body normally lets you sleep only the number of hours it needs, if you're going to bed too early, you will likely awake too early as well.

✔ **13** *Avoid naps, unless . . .*

James Perl, Ph.D., reports in the February/March 1994 *Remedy* article that "four out of five [people] with insomnia sleep better at night without naps." If you're a committed napper who also has insomnia, Perl suggests the following: "If you nap, skip [all naps] for a week. If you feel better and sleep better, then drop them. Or if you don't nap and want to see if they help you sleep better, take one before 3 p.m. each day for a week and not for more than an hour. Expect the total time you sleep at night to be reduced by the amount you nap in the day."

✔ **14** *Take a warm bath within two hours before bedtime.*

A 20-minute, warm, soaking bath of about 100°–102° not only is a great relaxer at day's end, but it also raises your core body temperature by several degrees. The ensuing drop in body temperature over the next two hours will naturally initiate drowsiness and sleep. In fact, a bath creates the same sleep-inducing, temperature-lowering effects that exercising five to six hours before bedtime does—although, of course, without improving your level of fitness.

✔ **15** *Don't obsess about sleep.*

Concentrating on when and if you're going to fall asleep can give you performance anxiety, making sleep that much more elusive. A 1985 study offered volunteers $25 if they could fall asleep quickly. It took them twice the time to fall asleep than it took other volunteers who were not under pressure to sleep. Anyone in the throes of a bout of insomnia knows that falling asleep is easier said than done; indeed, what *is* easy to do is obsess about being unable to sleep! If such fears roil your mind when you're in bed, try one of the relaxation methods we describe later. If that doesn't work after 20 minutes, get up and go to another room to do quiet reading or meditating until you are sleepy again.

✔ **16** *Adopt a good sleeping posture.*

Good posture in bed consists of sleeping in a modified "S" shape on your side, a small pillow under your head, another between your knees. Normally, says Dianne Hales in *How to Sleep Like a Baby*,* "your spine should maintain the same contours as when you are standing: chin, stomach, pelvis tucked in." People who snore (especially those with sleep apnea) are usually advised to sleep on their sides in

*New York: Ballantine Books, 1987.

order to keep their windpipes as unobstructed as possible. Keep in mind, however, that different musculoskeletal conditions—for instance, back problems—may dictate different sleep positions. Check with your practitioner.

✔ 17 Train your bladder to let you sleep.

Quentin Regestein, in *Sleep: Problems and Solutions*,* tells how: "Gradually prolong the time between your first urge to urinate and relieving yourself during the day, increasing the interval 15 minutes each week until it reaches a full 90 minutes. Then drink an extra 20 ounces of water [in the] mornings, but no liquids after supper in the evening." No one's going to tell you it's healthy for the bladder or kidneys to wait five more hours before you urinate if you feel the urge at 2 a.m. But this exercise—used to help those with incontinence problems—may buy you some additional time.

On a similar note: Try moving around for at least 10 minutes before lying down. Movement gets fluid into the bladder, and then you urinate before bed.

*New York: Consumers Union, 1990.

✔ **18 Sleep apart while you work out your sleeping problem.**

Couples who are used to sharing a bed actually sleep longer and better when they sleep alone, according to a 1994 British study. The research followed bed-sharing couples and then tracked the partners when they slept alone. Even though the couples said they felt they slept better together, the actual research—conducted using sleep logs and wristwatch-like devices that measured movements—showed that those who slept without a mate moved less and generally had more restful sleep. Half of all movements by one sleeper triggered moves by the other within 30 seconds. (An average adult sleeper changes sleeping positions anywhere between 20 and 60 times a night, or up to seven times an hour in a normal eight-hour night.) The research also found that men are more restless than women during sleep, and older couples are less affected by a partner's movements than younger couples.

✔ **19 Don't sleep with your pets.**

While your cat or dog may feel warm and cuddly nestled down by your feet, sleep research shows that having pets on the bed can be a sleep disrupter.

Sleep Environment

✔ **20** *Improve your sleep environment.*

By sleep environment, we mean everything that surrounds you or that you use when sleeping.

• **Lighting:** If you are a light-sensitive insomniac or if you work a night shift and must sleep in the daytime, consider black-out shades (like those found in better hotels, these are extra heavy, opaque shades that darken a room) and thick draperies or interior shutters at the windows. As a backup, keep a night mask—available at most drugstores—nearby. You may also want to dim (or cover) clocks or radio faces that glow in the dark.

• **Colors:** While pale colors—specifically, blues and greens—are considered cool, passive, and nonengaging, the color of your bedroom should be one that you like and don't find irritating; the color should be restful enough to help promote sleep.

• **Mattress:** You spend about a third of your life on one, so be sure you like it. Your size, health problems, and whether you share your bed with another person are key factors when choosing a mattress.

Size: Mattresses ideally should be at least six inches longer than you are tall. Width is a matter of personal preference, but consider that if two

adults share a standard double (full) bed, they are
sleeping in the same width of space (27″) allocated to
an infant in a crib! A restless sleeper should consider
queen-size as the smallest choice, with a king-size
bed a possibility. If one of you wakes easily when the
other moves, think about a king frame and box spring
supporting two twin mattresses joined by a foam bed
bridge (so you don't slip between the cracks). An individual's movements—which can wake up a bed-
mate who's a light sleeper—are felt less with this
arrangement.

Texture, firmness, noisiness: Choose from standard coil mattresses and box springs, platform beds
with foam mattress pads, or several kinds of water
beds. Older people or the very thin—who have less
natural padding and who may have to accommodate
health conditions like osteoporosis or painful
arthritis—may wish to add a quilted texture on the
mattress top to help soften the mattress. Others—
especially those with lower-back problems, who especially need musculoskeletal support—will want the
firmest mattress available. Willibald Nagler, M.D.,
chief of physiatry at New York Hospital–Cornell University Medical Center, believes that "99.9 percent of
the population would sleep better on a firm mattress
than a soft one. This holds true for back pain suffer-
ers especially. A soft mattress allows the back muscles to become overextended, which prevents them
from getting the rest they need. A firm mattress, on

the other hand, allows the back muscles to keep the spine in a more restful alignment."*

To check for noisiness, lie down and turn over with your ear to the mattress. If you can "hear" every move you make, this mattress will keep you awake better than a noisy neighbor. Clearly, trying out your mattress vigorously in the store before you buy is a good idea.

• **Pillows:** Personal preference and your state of health dictate a standard-size firm or soft pillow, a cervical or contour pillow (used by those with neck, back, and sleep apnea problems), or a foam or feather (down) pillow. Feather pillows feel soft and luxurious but set off allergic reactions (and subsequent sleeplessness) in many. The advantage of foam- or urethane-filled pillows is their washability.

• **Sheets and blankets:** Sheets should be comfortable, not too rough (180-thread is the coarsest you should choose, 200-thread feels better, and 250-or-more-thread is elegant). Silk or satin sheets may be good to look at but feel too slippery or cold to allow comfortable sleep, while flannel sheets may be too hot. Check to see if your blankets are the right weight for the season, and don't choose wool if you're allergic to natural wool fibers.

*Feltman, John, ed. *Prevention's How-To Dictionary of Healing Remedies and Techniques.* Emmaus, Pa.: Rodale Press, 1992.

• **Sleep attire:** If you have trouble sleeping, minimize such irritants as tight (or any) elastic at the waist, ankles, or wrists, and buttons or other fasteners that wake you when you roll on them. Also avoid fabrics that are too coarse.

• **Noise:** Noise, from inside and outside your home, even noise that you think you're so used to you don't hear anymore, may be contributing to your sleep woes. One famous sleep-noise study took place in residences near an airport, where occupants insisted they had grown so accustomed to aircraft landing and taking off that it no longer bothered them. (They insisted they didn't even hear the planes anymore.) Administered as they slept, the test proved them wrong. While they were not conscious of the plane noise, their brain wave changes reflected every takeoff and landing. Researchers concluded they were getting at least one full hour less of sleep a night than they thought they were getting.

Conversely, a steady, low sound—a low- or medium-speed setting on a fan, the low whir of an air conditioner, or the staticlike quality of a white noise machine—can soothe as well as block out other louder, sudden sounds and can contribute to better sleep. Also, consider installing thick carpeting that can soak up extraneous and loud noises. And be sure you eliminate these three bedroom electronics that can be distracting if you are a light sleeper: a ticking clock, a radio with a noisy mechanism, and a phone whose ring is a guaranteed end to sleep. Keep a pair of earplugs (sold at most drugstores) handy, in case all else fails; they should muffle the irritating sleep-retarding sounds but not the shrill noise of a smoke detector.

• **Ventilation:** It's conducive to good sleep to have some air movement in your bedroom, even if it's not fresh air coming through an open window. Consider installing a quiet, overhead paddle fan that has winter and summer settings to help with air movement.

• **Moisture:** Relative bedroom humidity between 60 and 70 percent (all year round) is optimal for keeping your skin conditioned and mucous membranes in your throat and nose from drying out. Having a whole-house humidifier installed on your furnace (forced air heating) or using a humidifier in your bedroom (especially in winter when it's drier) can help your immune system and breathing since your nose is less likely to be congested when you're trying to sleep. In the summer, a mean humidity of 60 to 70 percent (sometimes necessitating an air conditioner if you live in a humid, hot climate) can improve sleep by keeping you from getting sweaty and warm.

• **Temperature:** Research suggests that the ideal nighttime bedroom temperature is 60° to 65°F. The temperature should not be so cool that, in the middle of the night when your own body temperature drops to its lowest (during your longest REM sleep when you can't move, sweat, or shiver), you wake up freezing and grabbing for extra blankets. On the other hand, a bedroom that's too hot can hinder restful sleep. It may keep you awake longer and, once you are asleep, disturb your delta (deep) and REM sleep stages.

• **Cleanliness:** Aside from maintaining a dust-free bedroom to minimize allergic reactions, take a look around your bedroom and truly see what "message" it's conveying to you. If you're experiencing insomnia (especially if it's tied at all to stress or your inability to leave your daytime world behind when you sleep), keeping an uncluttered, "peaceful" bedroom setting is crucial. Not that you can't have beloved knickknacks or photos around you—you should be comfortable in your bedroom, after all—but try to resist an overabundance of items that set your mind racing: a desk stacked with unpaid bills, a bookcase or chair full of professional reading you need to do—all visual reminders of things that need attention. And be sure to get rid of items piled on the bed, too!

Lifestyle Choices

✔ **21** *Limit or avoid caffeine, especially after early afternoon.*

Caffeine, which the June 1993 *Consumer Reports on Health* calls "the most widely used drug in America," is a leading cause of short-term insomnia and often plays an important supporting role in various other sleep disorders. Caffeine is a stimulant that normally turns the mind on fast-forward and energizes it. Taken in excess, it can set the heart to racing, give you the jitters, or make you nauseated. Sensitivity to caffeine differs from person to person. Some coffee drinkers, for instance, need only a swallow or two of the brew to have an effect, while others can tolerate up to several cups without adverse reactions.

Normally, it takes the body three to five hours to clear out caffeine. In hypersensitive caffeine users, the substance can stick around for two or more times longer.

For most people, ingesting caffeine produces a reaction much like sugar does: It gives an instant "high," heightening alertness and lifting mood. When caffeine is ingested too late in the evening (within two hours of bedtime), it normally affects the ability to fall asleep. Regardless of what time it is ingested, caffeine taken in quantities of 300 milligrams a day (the equivalent of six or more cups of coffee or soft drinks a day) causes nighttime awakenings (of which the sleeper may not even be fully aware) and reduced periods of REM.

If you believe you are hypersensitive to caffeine, curtail intake of it from early afternoon on (assuming a bedtime at a normal hour).

Remember that caffeine is not limited to coffee, teas, and many of the darker-colored soft drinks, including Pepsi Cola and Coca-Cola Classic. It is also an ingredient of chocolate (the darker the chocolate, the more the caffeine) and assorted prescription and over-the-counter medications.

✔ 22 Modify your alcohol consumption.

It's a myth that alcohol—even a little—helps you sleep better. In reality, alcohol use is linked to a high percentage of sleep troubles. Alcohol fragments sleep. And alcohol rebound causes you to wake in the middle of the night. An April 1993 *McCall's* article recounts a study in which participants took several alcoholic drinks before bed. They slept deeply the first part of the night, but the rest of their sleep was so shallow that the next day their reaction times dropped by 10 percent. Experts recommend limiting your evening intake to one drink at least two hours before bed. (And depending on the nature of your sleeping problem, you may want to skip alcohol altogether.)

Even mild alcohol use in the evening can trigger or worsen snoring and sleep apnea; experts believe that alcohol worsens apnea by relaxing throat muscles and suppressing the brain's awakening mechanism, which adds time to how long it takes for the sleeper to stir and draw a breath.

✔ **23** Stop smoking and avoid secondhand smoke.

Low levels of nicotine can actually have a sedating effect, but as nicotine concentrations rise, the opposite effect is true: The smoker experiences arousal and agitation. A cigarette's half-life—the time the cigarette's chemicals take to clear out of your system—is one to two hours, so smoking just before bed can hinder sleep. A study of 3,500 people in Wisconsin, reported in the May 1994 *Preventive Medicine*, found that both male and female smokers had difficulty falling asleep and difficulty waking up (interestingly, only male smokers had nightmares and disturbing dreams). The study concluded that "sleep disturbances may be more prevalent among smokers due to stimulant effects of nicotine [and] nightly withdrawal," among other factors.

And there is conclusive evidence that heavy smokers often develop breathing difficulties, a common contributor to poor sleep.

✔ 24 Just say no!

Aside from all the other negative effects of illegal drugs, evidence suggests they only make sleep problems worse, according to *The Concise Guide to the Evaluation and Management of Sleep Disorders*.* And there is no evidence that they improve sleep. A look at four well-known illegal substances shows this: Heroin is a depressant that slows motor functions and breathing, which results in fragmented sleep and less deep sleep; amphetamines are stimulants that reduce delta (deep) and REM sleep (withdrawal creates REM rebound, which is highly sleep disruptive); cocaine's stimulating initial effects are followed quickly by depression, negatively affecting the sleep-wake cycle, dopamine production, and REM sleep; and marijuana alters the brain chemicals involved in sleep and decreases REM sleep.

✔ 25 Exercise regularly for good sleep.

Insomniacs who have trouble falling asleep often have body temperatures that stay higher longer into the night than other people's. Exercise can deepen the "trough" of your temperature range, influencing your core temperature to go lower, a factor that is tied to improving your most restorative sleep. Researchers at

*Reite, Martin L., and Kim Nagle. Washington, D.C.: American Psychiatric Press, 1990.

Duke University Medical Center, in Durham, North Carolina, examined sleep in healthy over-60 men, half of whom led sedentary lives. They found that the men who exercised fell asleep in half the time of their sedentary counterparts, slept longer, and had longer restorative sleep, according to a June 25, 1992, *Medical Tribune* article.

The best form of exercise is aerobic—continuous 20- to 30-minute sessions three to five times a week, consisting of repetitive motions that make your heart beat faster and speed up your breathing, preceded by 10 minutes of warm-ups and stretches. Besides the benefits to your cardiovascular system, exercise releases sleep-enhancing endorphins, the body chemicals that give you a feeling of well-being, relieve depression, and relax you. Don't overdo it, though. Sleep disturbance can be a sign of overtraining, according to a July 20, 1993, *Washington Post Health* article.

✔ 26 *Don't exercise too close to bedtime.*

The key here is body temperature, which normally is at its highest during the daytime and falls at night. When it starts falling, you get sleepy, less alert, less active. Your sleeping temperature is lower than your daytime temperature, and in your deepest sleep—for normal sleepers sometime between 2 and 4 a.m.— your temperature drops to its lowest level in 24 hours. Aerobic exercise of a 20-minute duration that raises your normal (core) temperature by two degrees will influence your body temperature to drop five to six hours after your exercise ends.

What this means for the insomniac is this: By exercising *five to six hours before bedtime*, you can engineer your dropping temperature to coincide with when you want to go to sleep.

✔ 27 Lose weight.

If you suffer from a sleep disorder and you're overweight, there just may be a connection. And if you eat fatty foods too close to bedtime, when you try to go to sleep you'll discover that your digestive system is still processing that last fatty meal, and you're likely to have an uncomfortable time getting to sleep or sleeping soundly when you do. (In fact, this is the case whether you're overweight or not.)

Further, if you eat too many fats and simple carbohydrates, the calories are not turned into the right kind and amount of energy you need. Without enough energy, everything—climbing, walking, digesting, even breathing as you try to sleep—becomes an effort that taxes your system. Overweight people also add the risk of developing severe sleep apnea (and snoring), since fat tissue in the throat and neck impedes correct breathing while they sleep.

The problem of excess weight and the sleep disruptions associated with it are at least partially correctable with self-care. Losing as little as 20 pounds should make you feel a difference, even in your sleep patterns, says Hales in *How to Sleep Like a Baby*.

✔ 28 Limber up your muscles and joints.

Adopting a regular movement-therapy program is not only critical to retaining your range of motion but is also essential for sound sleep, *especially* as you age. Arthritis can cause chronic, sleep-disrupting pain, marked by frequent awakenings and shallower—less restorative—sleep. Sleepers with chronic pain often awake every time they move. Studies have shown that when people are awoken every 10 minutes, their loss of restorative sleep is severe enough to represent an actual three to four hours of sleep loss. Work with your doctor or movement therapist to devise a toning program that accommodates any limits you may have.

✔ 29 Control seasonal allergies.

If you're one of the millions of Americans who are allergic to pollen, dust, mold, feathers, grasses, or pet hair, you can probably tell what month it is by how many times a night you wake up from a sinus headache or an inability to breathe. One option you have is to undergo a multiyear desensitization program of injections that reduce (but seldom eliminate fully) your body's reaction to the offending irritants. A successful shot regimen may make it possible for you to again sleep through a full night. Meanwhile, there are some effective home remedies you can employ to ease allergy-related sleeping problems: Keep your sleeping quarters dust-free by cleaning and vacuuming often. Avoid using dust-catching accoutrements, such as heavy draperies and bedspreads. Use pillows with synthetic filling and wash them often, just as you should wash your mattress pad frequently. Stay indoors at night (when pollen and mold spore counts are highest), and either sleep with your window closed or purchase a hypoallergenic filter for your window to help prevent pollen and other allergens from entering on the night air.

Diet and Nutrition

✔ **30** *Eat to sleep.*

Eating and sleeping are interconnected. As alluring as a late-night box of chocolate bonbons may sound, it can easily lead to a night of restless tossing and turning. Rich and/or highly spiced foods, for instance, make the digestive system work overtime when it should be gearing down for the night. While not all food and drink produce the same effect in all people, undoubtedly certain ones may keep *you* awake. Therefore, revisit what you ate at meals before nights you lay awake, wide-eyed, staring at the ceiling. Eliminate what you think might be the offender. After a few tries you may discover that a particular food is causing the problem.

✔ 31 Don't eat foods high in protein close to bedtime.

Consuming too much protein in the evening gives your brain the message that it's time to wake up and get busy. Absorbed more slowly than carbohydrates, proteins sustain energy longer, making them the body's best fatigue fighters. They also lead to the production of dopamine and epinephrine (adrenaline), the neurotransmitters associated with alertness and energy.

✔ 32 Eat carbohydrates to promote sleep.

Carbohydrates—sugars and starches—normally promote calm by stimulating conversion of the amino acid tryptophan into serotonin, the neurotransmitter that regulates sleep, reduces pain, appetite, and irritability, and elevates moods. Sugars fuel a quick energy high, followed by a crash, after which sleepy and lethargic feelings set in. Starches, the complex carbohydrates found in cereals, pasta, potatoes, and rice, take hold more slowly and last longer because the body doesn't absorb such carbohydrates as fast.

A high-carbohydrate breakfast will probably have no effect on your sleep patterns. However, what you eat for dinner and what you eat as a pre-bedtime snack are different matters. For the best sleep-promoting effects, dinner should be a light combination of complex carbohydrates and proteins (carbohydrates help offset the energy buzz that proteins provide), ideally at least four hours before you plan to go to sleep. A snack that consists mainly of complex carbohydrates—an English muffin, a bowl of cereal (but don't overdo the milk), wheat crackers—eaten one to two hours before bed has the most sedating effect on your sleep. You can use a little sugar or protein to add zest to your snack—a dab of jelly for your muffin, a small portion of low-fat milk for the cereal. But you don't want to wind up canceling out the carbohydrates' drowsiness-inducing actions.

✔ 33 Eat a big breakfast, a moderate lunch and a light dinner.

This way, your body gets the most calories during the day, when it needs energy. Regular timing is important, too, as we note above. Don't go to bed hungry, however. A growling stomach is as much a sleep buster as a too-full one.

✔ 34 Find out if you suffer from hypoglycemia.

If you wake up in the middle of the night, have a sweet tooth, and experience dramatic mood and energy swings, ask your doctor to check you for low blood sugar, or hypoglycemia. Hypoglycemia is a medical condition that needs to be treated by a doctor who can work with you on changing your eating patterns and diet. Partly the result of eating too many simple carbohydrates (sugars), hypoglycemia overstimulates insulin production, which zaps not only the sugar just eaten but also robs the bloodstream of glucose, leaving blood-sugar levels abnormally low. Since glucose is the brain's fuel, says Philip Goldberg, author of *Everybody's Guide to Natural Sleep*,* this depletion slows a person down and makes her extremely tired. This condition also disturbs normal sleep patterns, because the body reacts to a glucose shortage by entering into an emergency state and by speeding up secretion of emergency hormones. You can awake in the middle of night "bug-eyed and wired for action," in the words of Goldberg.

Low blood sugar can affect sleep another way, too. In *Sleep: Problems and Solutions*, Regestein says that, on the downswing from a quick sugar high, appetite picks up. People who eat lots of sugary snacks instead of meals often miss the timing cues the body gets from regular mealtimes, he says, and this throws off natural sleep rhythms.

*New York: St. Martin's Press, 1990.

✔ **35** When it's close to bedtime, avoid certain cheeses and other foods containing tyrosine.

Once in the body, the amino acid tyrosine converts to a substance that stimulates release of dopamine and noradrenaline, the neurotransmitters that energize your mind, make you attentive, and heighten your alertness—definitely not ingredients for good sleep. Tyrosine-rich foods, eaten too close to bedtime, can also trigger sleep-disrupting heart palpitations. Tyrosine-rich foods include aged cheeses, such as stilton, blue, and parmesan, and soft cheeses, such as mozzarella, Swiss, Gruyère, and feta. Tyrosine is also a component of red wine, yogurt, sour cream, cured and processed meats and fish, yeast products, eggplant, potatoes, spinach, and tomatoes.

Milk is packed with tyrosine and can have the unwanted effect of energizing you when you least need it. No one has a sound scientific idea of why warm milk—a recommended soporific—helps some people sleep: Even though it's laced with tryptophan, the amino acid that stimulates serotonin production, milk has too many other amino acids, according to most experts, for it to do much good with your serotonin volume. Jean Carper, in her book *Food: Your Miracle Medicine*,* notes that MIT researchers now believe

*New York: HarperCollins, 1993.

drinking milk is more likely to wake people than to put them to sleep due to its protein (fatigue-fighting) content. But she goes on to recount other recent studies that show milk contains natural opiates thought to cause drowsiness.

Bottom line? If drinking milk before bed helps you fall asleep, do it.

✔ **36** *Eat foods and herbs with calming, sedative properties.*

Herbals and botanicals have been used through the centuries to treat insomnia. Carper nominates anise, celery seed, clove, cumin, fennel, garlic, ginger, honey, lime peel, marjoram, onion, orange peel, parsley, sage, spearmint, sugar, and decaffeinated tea as nature's mild sedatives and tranquilizers. Other experts include catnip, lady's slipper, chamomile, passionflower, skullcap, and valerian root in the sleep-aid list. Buy herbals and botanicals in health-food stores, through mail order, and in some supermarkets.

Insomnia-abating herbals are often taken in the form of tea shortly (one authority says 45 minutes) before bedtime. *The Magic and Medicine of Plants** provides this handy formula: Use one to three teaspoons of the dried herb (depending upon your personal taste and strength of tea desired), steeped five

*Dobelis, Inge, et al. Pleasantville, N.Y.: Reader's Digest Books, 1993.

minutes in one cup of water that has been boiled (as opposed to steeping it in water currently over a heat source).

Remember: Just because herbals and botanicals are natural and unregulated by the Food and Drug Administration does not mean they can't be harmful. Before you use them, ask and read about them, then carefully follow instructions for their use. Be especially alert to rare but potent side effects; for instance, herbals are not recommended for those with hay fever or other plant allergies. People with high blood pressure are warned against certain herbals that can raise blood pressure—gentian, ginseng, juniper, and licorice, according to *Rodale's Illustrated Encyclopedia of Herbs.**

✔ 37 *Drink valerian tea before bedtime.*

Forty-five minutes before bedtime, try a cup of valerian or passionflower tea. Hailed for their sedative effects, both folk medicines have been around for centuries. In particular, valerian is said to improve sleep onset and sleep quality. Indeed, valerian (available in health-food stores and catalogs) is the over-the-counter tranquilizer of choice in much of Europe, where herbal medicine is more widely practiced than in this country. Valerian is nonaddictive and, if taken in a moderate dose (two teaspoons per cup of boiling

*Emmaus, Pa.: Rodale Press, 1987.

water), leaves no morning-after grogginess. Overuse, however, can give you headaches, nausea, and grogginess.* For either tea, use one to two grams from dried roots or one-half to one teaspoon fluid extract in a cup of boiling water.†

✔ 38 Get enough B-complex vitamins daily.

Aside from fighting stress, maintaining the nervous system, and avoiding fatigue, B-complex vitamins are helpful for good sleep. However, these vitamins affect different people differently: They energize some and sedate others. If you're eating regular, nutritious meals, you may be getting the full recommended dietary allowances of these vitamins in your food. If not, often just adding a good multivitamin to your daily regimen is all it takes. Megadosing is not recommended and may even be harmful.

Below are the pertinent B-complex vitamins, their roles in good sleep, and their natural sources. (Recommended dietary allowances [RDAs] for 25- to 50-year-old women and men appear in parentheses.)

• **Niacin (B₃):** Helps improve insomnia-related depression; increases effectiveness of tryptophan by maintaining adequate blood levels of serotonin (neurotransmitter that regulates sleep); prolongs REM

---

*Feltman, *Prevention's How-To Dictionary.*
†Murray, Michael, N.D., and Joseph Pizzorno, N.D. *The Encyclopedia of Natural Medicine.* Rocklin, Ca.: Prima Publishing, 1991.

sleep; can reduce an insomniac's "awake time." Food sources: brewer's yeast, wheat bran, peanuts, chicken and turkey, tuna, beef, whole-wheat products. Fruits, vegetables, and dairy products all contain some. (13–19 mg.)

• **Cobalamin (B_{12}):** Helps establish normal sleep-wake cycles in those who have difficulty falling asleep and who experience frequent awakenings. Average adult gets enough in diet, but new studies show those over 65 often have too low a level due to intestinal malabsorption problems. Food sources: liver and organ meats, muscle meats, fish, eggs, shellfish, milk and most dairy products, but not butter. (2 mcg.)

• **Folic Acid:** Helps with fatigue and some forms of insomnia, including restless-leg syndrome, associated with folic acid deficiency. Food sources: liver, brewer's yeast, dark green leafy vegetables (like spinach), dried beans, green vegetables, lettuce and broccoli, fresh oranges, whole-wheat products. (Women: 180 mcg.; men: 200 mcg.)

• **Pantothenic acid:** Helps sleep disturbances associated with deficiency. Food sources: brewer's yeast, liver, eggs, wheat germ and bran, peanuts and peas, meats, milk, poultry, whole grains, broccoli, mushrooms, sweet potatoes. (No RDA but an estimated safe and adequate daily dietary intake is 4–7 mg.)

• **Pyridoxine (B_6):** Is necessary for conversion of tryptophan to serotonin. Many people appear to get too little in regular diets. Food sources: chicken, fish, liver, kidney, pork and eggs, brown rice, soybeans, oats, whole-wheat products, peanuts, walnuts. (Women: 1.6 mg.; men: 2 mg.)

✔ **39** Make sure you're getting enough of the minerals calcium, magnesium, copper, and iron.

Inadequate amounts of calcium and magnesium in your diet can cause you to wake up after only a few hours of sleep and not be able to return to sleep, according to James F. Balch, M.D., author of *Prescription for Nutritional Healing.** Food sources: Calcium—milk and dairy products, kale and turnip greens, canned salmon, and soybeans. (Most experts agree that *at least* 800 mg. for men and women is needed to maintain health; others prescribe at least 1,000 mg./day. Calcium supplements should be accompanied by magnesium and potassium to help absorption.)

Insomniacs who have been helped by magnesium supplements have been able to fall asleep more quickly, enjoy uninterrupted sleep, and awake refreshed, and takers notice less tension and anxiety during waking hours, reports Mayo Clinic's Peter Hauri, Ph.D., in *No More Sleepless Nights*. Natural foods all contain some magnesium, but best food

*Garden City Park, N.Y.: Avery, 1990.

sources are: legumes, nuts, whole grains, and shell-fish. (RDAs for men: 350 mg.; for women: 300 mg. Some nutritionists recommend a higher dosage, but magnesium should be taken in a ratio to calcium of 1:2.)

A deficiency of either copper or iron or both has been shown to decrease sleep quality. Studies by the U.S. Department of Agriculture of copper-deficient persons found that they slept longer but felt worse when they awoke. People who were iron-deficient slept longer, too, but they awoke more during the night. Food sources: Copper—nuts, organ meats, sea-food, mushrooms, chocolate, and legumes. Food sources: Iron—liver, heart, kidney, lean meats, shell-fish, dried beans and fruits, nuts, and green leafy veg-etables. (RDAs: copper: 2–3 mg.; iron: 10–18 mg.)

A word of caution: Many authorities advise against supplementing copper and/or iron on your own. Dominick Bosco, author of *The People's Guide to Vitamins and Minerals*,* warns that what constitutes adequate copper and iron amounts is a delicate bal-ance that requires the help of a trained professional. If the scale tilts either way—deficiency or excess—it can affect the quality of sleep, at the very least, and may have other, more serious side effects.

*Chicago: Contemporary Books, 1989.

Mind-Body Connection

✔ **40** *Eliminate or lessen the unhealthy stress in your life.*

Not dealing effectively with bad stress is a leading cause of insomnia. Often called "fight or flight syndrome," the body's stress response is nature's way of raising the nervous system's sensitivities and reflexes to meet short-term emergencies. The response cues the nervous system to pump adrenaline into the blood, speeding up heart rate and making hands and feet clammy and cold, breathing shallow, and muscles flexed at the ready. Chronic, or prolonged, stress is unhealthy because stress chemicals keep pumping into the system but the body can no longer restore its energy reserves; consequently, exhaustion (and insomnia) set in.

A sleep log (described earlier) may generate important clues to help you identify specific causes of bad stress. Note what activities, emotions, topics of concern, and personal interactions you listed for the days and evenings immediately preceding your bad nights. Are there any patterns or repetitions you might not have considered before?

✔ **41** *Relax.*

For good sleep, you need to relax away your stress throughout the day, not just before bedtime. True relaxation doesn't happen spontaneously, and it doesn't mean doing nothing. It's a learned skill that anyone can acquire through practice.

Here are 11 of the better-known relaxation techniques suggested by leading sleep therapists. Find one (or more!) that works for you.

• **Progressive muscle relaxation:** an exercise appropriate for bedtime. Close your eyes and, starting from your feet, visualize one group of muscles at a time, relaxing each along the way. Continue until you have "moved through" your entire body and/or feel the tension depart and a feeling of weightlessness set in.

• **Deep breathing:** the classic tension-relieving exercise, to be done at intervals during the day and again at bedtime, sitting up or lying down. Pull shoulders back as you inhale, feeling air fill your diaphragm. Hold for three seconds. Exhale, letting shoulders drop. Repeat until you feel less tense.

• **Distraction therapy:** a method in which you focus your attention on where tension accumulates in your body—neck and shoulders, for instance—then alternate tensing and relaxing. Alternating helps you recognize muscle groups. Commercial audio- and videotapes are available; check with your local video store or library.

• **Autogenic training:** another progressive muscle relaxation strategy, in which you concentrate on repetitive phrases ("My feet are getting heavy, my legs are getting heavy"). The phrases emphasize a feeling of heaviness and relaxation in different parts of your body. Commercial audio- and videotapes are available.

• **Meditation:** a consciousness-altering exercise done ideally three times daily (morning, afternoon, early evening), to clear your mind and heighten your awareness of involuntary body rhythms, such as breathing and heart rate. You repeat to yourself a special sound (mantra) that you select, allowing it to come and go while you are comfortably seated, eyes closed, for 20 minutes. Successful meditation is said to lower blood pressure and heart rate and slow the breathing.

• **Relaxation response:** a method, developed by a cardiologist, to be done three times a day (for 20 minutes each time), including bedtime. Select one short word to repeat to yourself, letting it slip out of mind easily if something else appears. Once you "see" it is gone, focus to bring it back: This process helps you learn mind-centered control in order to leave behind stress and specific worries.

• **Yoga:** a meditative movement therapy; one or two sessions are recommended daily, along with some stretches just before bed. Yoga relieves stress through regulation of body posture, gentle exercise, ability to direct concentration, and repetition of a mantra. Successful yoga enthusiasts say they attain complete body and mind mastery. Commercial audio- and videotapes are available.

• **Biofeedback:** a relaxation strategy using the human mind to influence and, to a certain extent, control the autonomic nervous system of the body— the involuntary system that regulates heartbeat, blood circulation, and the action of the digestive system. In this case the goal is to switch your brain waves from beta (stressed) to alpha (calm). Biofeedback can be self-taught or learned in a behavioral lab. Mayo Clinic's Peter Hauri, Ph.D., notes that EMG biofeedback, which measures electrical currents generated in muscles, can help the more aroused, hyper type of insomniac. Sensorimotor (SMR) biofeedback helps a person attain and maintain a particular brain rhythm and is used mostly with those who wake in the night and who are not tense.

• **Cognitive focusing:** a bedtime strategy to turn off the racing brain. It employs use of imagery to focus the mind and help it relax. Cognitive focusing consists of positive concentration on something you want (like falling back asleep); thinking with hope ("If I want it to be so, it will be so"); breathing deeply; and repeating calm thoughts silently to self. Also called **cognitive refocusing**.

• **Stimulus control**: a relaxation process in which you condition yourself to associate bed with rest, go to bed only when sleepy, and don't engage in any other activities in the bedroom (such as reading, knitting, watching TV). If you don't sleep within 10 minutes, you get up and leave the bedroom and don't come back until you're sleepy. Do this as often as needed until you fall asleep within 10 minutes. Other important tenets in this process: Regardless of how little you sleep, rise at a set time; don't nap; keep a careful record of progress.

• **Paradoxical intention**: a bedtime strategy in which you try to stay awake. In a Temple University study, writes Hales in *How to Sleep Like a Baby*, insomniacs who had failed at other relaxation techniques were told that study directors needed more information on participants' presleep thoughts. They were thereby instructed to stay awake as long as possible. Most fell asleep 50 percent faster. Study leaders speculated the insomniacs view night as a high-anxiety test. Once the pressure's off, they can sleep.

✔ **42** *Recognize the early warning signs of burnout and take action.*

Constant stress and pressure make you an ideal candidate for burnout, a totally exhausted state marked by insomnia, digestion problems, an inability to feel refreshed, muscle aches, and colds. The good news is that burnout is reversible, if caught in time. Recognize these early warning signs: feeling disinterested in your job or hobby or relationship; lacking energy to face the day; being too bored or too tired to tackle the job or situation; feeling like there's no way to recapture the excitement or challenge you once felt about a job, relationship, or activity.

As for what you can do, one expert* recommends that you (1) spend daily time—even 30 minutes—on yourself; (2) do something totally different from what is exhausting you; (3) examine what you do and how—it may not be the *what* that's getting to you, but the *way* you do it that needs to be changed; (4) test your priorities against what's overtaxing you to see if they're in conflict, and revise priorities, if necessary; (5) consider your motives for why you are exposing yourself to burnout (are you fixating on your job to avoid dealing with problematic family relationships?); (6) examine, maintain, and strengthen your ties to friends and family, your support system; (7) don't do the job alone—insist on help or delegate work; and (8) eat, (try to) sleep, and be merry—well-balanced meals, rest, and diversion are critical for better perspective.

*Bell, *Chronic Fatigue.*

✔ 43 Set realistic goals and deadlines.

The unrealistic goal setter is never ready for bed because the list is never finished, the job is never right, the deadline is never met. If you're a high-achieving personality drawing up the daily to-do list, you may be inviting chronic stress and continued insomnia without realizing it. Reverse the trend by reviewing your goals and deadlines. Are they too ambitious? Are you trying to achieve too much in the time you've allocated? Are you afraid to say no? If so, why? Evaluate the worst that could happen if you were to modify your goals and deadlines. Then try it.

✔ 44 "Suboptimize."

Studies show that many people who have chronic insomnia at night are perfectionists during the day. Let part of your stress-reduction efforts include a commitment to suboptimize, as some management consultants call it—to accept less than perfection of yourself and others. People who expect perfection are rarely happy with any results, and that adds stress, tension, fatigue, and overload to any situation.

Here are a few tricks of the trade for suboptimizing: (1) Choose what projects you're doing that do not have to be perfect; (2) delegate some (or all) of the job, even when you know it will not be done as well by someone else; (3) allow yourself to fail occasionally (it's the only way we can let ourselves take risks and learn); and (4) review priorities—everything doesn't demand equal attention.

✔ 45 Don't worry, be happy.

Writing in the November 1993 *Prevention*, Cathy Perlmutter notes, "Chronic worriers tend to focus on a variety of problems without finding solutions for any. . . . Most people worry 5 percent of the time, but chronic worriers may spend 50 to 100 percent of their time worrying." Restless sleep is often the bothersome result. Ways to reform chronic worrying include learning more effective problem-solving techniques and identifying the worries that are beyond control. Learning to focus on the present is another way to break out of what is probably a lifelong habit of worrying. One of the biggest challenges a chronic worrier must face to get a handle on better sleep is to feel in control (again). Research reported in the July/August 1993 *Psychology Today* shows that happy people, who tend to enjoy restful sleep, share these characteristics: feelings of personal control, high self-esteem, optimism, extroversion, and enjoyment of living in the present. The article suggests that learning how to lose yourself in work or hobbies to stimulate happy feelings is a good start toward being happier—and sleeping better.

Another tactic is to assign time to worries, then table them. Plan a specific time to take on your worries. In 15 to 30 minutes, write down all of your nagging worries. Review the list and cross off the anxieties over which you have no control. With those remaining, make notes on which items can be solved in the immediate future and which will take longer. Spend the last few minutes jotting down possible solutions and a realistic timetable for accomplishing them. When your allotted time is up, put your list away until the next day, when you can then work on the short-term items if you wish.

✔ 46 *Laugh.*

A good belly laugh stimulates the release of endorphins, hormones that tell us we are feeling good, give us a natural high, and relax us enough to go to sleep. Conversely, anger and its by-products diminish the effects of these good hormones, while overwhelming the body with bad chemicals that flood the stomach with acid and launch headaches and even sleeplessness.

✔ 47 *Determine if your insomnia is due to depression.*

Depression can play tricks on your sleep patterns. Some depressed people sleep too much, suffering constant fatigue, and are often unable even to rise out of bed. But another indicator of depression is debilitating insomnia, characteristically experienced by waking in the middle of the night and not being able to get back to sleep. In a depressed person, insomnia is usually accompanied by any or all of these other symptoms: feelings of hopelessness and despair, low self-esteem, unusual lethargy, and/or suicidal thoughts. If you think there's even a small chance you may be suffering from depression, see your doctor without delay. Leaving depression untreated is almost a sure bet that your sleep deficit will increase until it may become intolerable. Extreme fatigue clouds a person's ability to think straight and is often a factor in suicide.

Circadian Connection

✔ **48** *Lighten up your jet lag.*

Jet lag disrupts more than 100 different bodily functions, according to Robert M. Giller, M.D., in *Natural Prescriptions.** For reasons scientists don't fully understand yet, flying west toward lengthened days is easier on your system than flying east, which shortens your day. Circadian research suggests that most people need one day of adjustment for every time zone they pass.

Here are a few strategies to minimize jet lag and its debilitating effects on your sleep:

*New York: Carol Southern Books, 1994.

• **Clock therapy (chronotherapy):** In *Chronic Fatigue*, Bell gives this advice to travelers: (1) Stay calm while preparing for the trip, to ensure a relaxed departure. (2) Start to reset your biological clock five days before you leave: If flying east, start going to bed and waking earlier each day; if heading west, stay up and get up later. (3) Reset your watch when you get on the plane. While airborne, try to eat and sleep according to the new schedule, in spite of the airline's imposed schedule. (4) Don't drink alcohol or caffeine on the flight (both are diuretics and increase fatigue), but instead stick to water and juices. (5) Consider using medications, either antihistamines to induce sleep or short-acting sleeping pills that won't cause a hangover. (6) Don't spend the first eight hours in bed once you arrive. If you arrive in daytime, take a short nap before going out in the sun (sunlight stops the melatonin production that makes you sleepy). (7) Don't overdo your schedule the first couple of days you're there. You should also resume your exercise program on arrival.

• **Light therapy (phototherapy):** After flying west across fewer than seven time zones, spend time outdoors at the end of each day, advises the March 1994 *Consumer Reports on Health*. After you've flown west across seven or more time zones, get mid-day light. After flying east across fewer than seven time zones, go outdoors early in the day. After you've flown east and crossed seven or more time zones, get midday light.

✔ 49 *Drink a lot of water during airplane travel, to help offset the sleep disruptions that jet lag causes.*

Airplane cabins are notorious for their dehydrating effects on the body, and dehydration is thought to accentuate problems your body's systems undergo adjusting to time-zone changes. A quick reminder: While flying, avoid caffeine and alcohol, as both dehydrate and further stress your body, and both interfere with sleep.

✔ 50 *Be alert to these pointers if you're a shift worker.*

You may not know the technical name, *circadian-cycle disturbances*, but if you're a shift worker you're familiar with the insomnia that results. Here are strategies to deal with this work-related condition:

To start with, if you're working one-week rotations in a day (7–3) to late night (11–7) to evening (3–11) pattern, talk to your employer about lengthening shift assignments to three weeks each and rotating them in a forward, sequential—day to evening to night—progression. Research shows that it's easier for most people (particularly those age 55 and under) to "phase advance" their internal clocks by moving to longer days than it is to "phase delay" their schedules by moving backward. Studies have also shown that resetting circadian rhythm takes three to four weeks to complete the adjustment.

And don't forget:

• Employ all possible techniques to sound- and light-proof your bedroom.

• Exercise every day, but do it after you've slept, not immediately before.

• Eat high-protein meals before work and high-carbohydrate meals before you sleep.

• Prepare for your new sleep schedule on your days off before the shift changes. When the next shift is an evening shift, stay up a little later and sleep later in the morning.

✔ 51 *Get more sunlight.*

You need sunlight or its equivalent every day. "Sleep troubles are disproportionately more common among those who spend more of their time indoors," writes Perl in the February/March 1994 *Remedy*. Perl and others note that blind persons often have the same troubles as the housebound: Sunlight cues are not picked up through the eyes to tell the brain's inner clock to sleep or wake. Scientists believe that humans were designed as diurnal, not nocturnal, beings, destined to carry out most of our functions in daytime—hence our sensitivity to light as an energy source.

By exposing yourself to strong light, you influence the secretion of melatonin, the light-sensitive hormone that regulates sleep. Sunlight or equivalently strong light (2,500 lux or more) can be used to manipulate and change our sleep-wake cycles by delaying or advancing them. If you wake up too early, stay indoors before about 10 a.m. or, if you must go outside, wear sunglasses. And get outside as much as possible during the last several hours of daylight, suggests the March 1994 *Consumer Reports on Health.* Conversely, if you can't wake up until late morning, set your alarm and plan to spend time outside as early as possible (30 minutes after sunrise is ideal but before 10 a.m. is essential) and avoid outdoor light in the late afternoon or evening.

✔ 52 Reset your body clock if you're waking up too early.

If you're an early-morning riser who's going to bed too early, you may suffer from the type of insomnia known as *advanced-phase sleep disorder*, also known as *early-waking insomnia.* You can reset your clock in two different ways:

• Use light therapy to reset your body clock. "If you wake up in the middle of the night and can't go back to sleep, expose yourself to extra sunlight late in the afternoon and avoid any extra early-morning light," counsels a September 1992 *Health* article. *Consumer Reports on Health* advises: "Wear dark glasses or stay indoors before 10 a.m. Then get outside as much as possible during the last several hours of daylight."

Research shows that bright-light treatment—using sunlight or bright artificial light—should be given every day for two to four hours, depending on the intensity of light and level of insomnia, for one month to obtain maximum benefit. It can then be reduced to a session every two to three days to sustain the improvement. (A number of experts believe that using light brighter than the equivalent of early-morning light could cut the length of sessions to 30 minutes.) Two recent studies employing such light therapy resulted in volunteers being able to sleep an hour longer each day than untreated volunteers. Bright-light treatment should not be tried without the advice of your doctor, however.

• Chronotherapy can also reset your clock. Let's say you're falling asleep at 7:30 p.m. and waking up at 3:30 a.m. If you want to make 11 p.m. your new bedtime (which should allow you to sleep until 7 a.m.), you will need to take two weeks in which you "back around the clock," advancing your bedtime by three hours every two days—going to bed at 4:30 p.m., 1:30 p.m., 10:30 a.m., until you get to your new 11 p.m. bedtime. Don't take naps while you are resetting your clock. And once you have reached the desired bedtime, you must be vigilant about sticking to it—or you will have to start over. Chronotherapy takes diligence and understanding, not only from you, as you move through bizarre bedtimes, but from those around you. This relatively short retraining period works to solve many insomnia cases.

✔ **53** *Reset your body clock if you're a night owl.*

Night owls classically have body temperatures that don't peak until early evening, which pushes their natural bedtimes to the middle of the night and awaking times to anywhere from late morning to midday. For these people, who suffer from delayed-phase sleep disorder, most of the insomnia therapies—relaxation techniques, cognitive focusing, and restriction therapy—don't work, according to Mayo Clinic's Peter Hauri, nor does arbitrarily setting an earlier bedtime without other accompanying treatment. For this particular problem, a night owl needs a plan of attack that ultimately results in setting earlier bed- and rising times.

• To use light therapy, spend time outdoors as early in the day as daylight makes it possible, but always before 10 a.m., says *Consumer Reports on*

Health, adding: "Avoid outdoor light in the late afternoon or evening." If bright, artificial indoor light is used, light sessions should parallel the same times of day you would otherwise be outside.

• To reestablish earlier bed- and rising times, select an earlier desired bedtime—say 11 p.m. Then move forward around the clock in increments until you reach 11 p.m. For example, if you are currently going to sleep at 3 a.m. and arising at 11 a.m., your first readjusted bedtime would be at 6 a.m., the next at 9 a.m., then noon, until you get back to 11 p.m. (While some therapists advise resetting your clock this way in as little as a week, others recommend staying with each new bedtime for at least two days at a time. "If you're really susceptible," suggests *New York Times* health writer Jane Brody in an April 24, 1994, article, "slow it to over six to seven weeks, with a three-hour step per week.")

New Research

✔ **54 Keep abreast of the latest developments regarding sleep.**

• . . . **On melatonin:** New studies in the United States and in Britain indicate that for circadian-related insomnia, the synthetic hormone melatonin may be the traveler's pill of the future—a sleep-regulating substance that can help reset body clocks and markedly decrease jet lag and tiredness after long flights. Indeed, some scientists believe that melatonin may become a major, natural, nonaddictive sleeping aid used to promote healthy sleep cycles, according to a June 1993 *Harvard Health Letter* report.

Writing about melatonin in the April 1994 *Condé Nast Traveler*, Richard Dawood, M.D., notes that in studies on volunteers who took melatonin after transmeridian flights, the best results were obtained when 5 to 10 mg. of melatonin were taken 30 to 90 minutes before bedtime, starting on the night of arrival and discontinuing as soon as signs of jet lag disappeared. Deviating a bit from that advice, in the October 1994 *Esquire*, writer Michael Segell suggests, "Taking a small dose in the morning delays sleep, while a little in the afternoon seems to promote sleepiness."

Although legal, self-medicating with synthetic melatonin in this country is currently controversial. Synthetic melatonin has been a staple of health-food stores for years, but not until recent clinical studies has the medical community recognized it and begun calling upon the Food and Drug Administration to regulate it as a drug. Studies to date on synthesized melatonin's sleep-regulating properties have shown it to be universally efficacious in modulating certain circadian-related disruptions like jet lag. Other than a mild contraceptive effect on some women, according to Dawood, synthetic melatonin appears to have few if any known side effects. (Natural melatonin, however, produces lightening of the skin and plays a role in sexual development, according to Segell, so there may be much more to learn about possible side effects.)

While hailing melatonin as a probable hangover-free sleep drug of the next decade, doctors continue to be cautious. They are quick to warn that, as an unregulated substance, synthesized melatonin could be impure or arrive on market shelves in varying strengths. Meanwhile, scores of long-distance travelers are turning away from short-effect sleeping pills and buying 3 mg. melatonin supplements at health-food stores. If you're interested in trying melatonin supplementation for a particular sleep problem, we advise that you check with your doctor—and keep abreast of continuing scientific developments.

• . . . **On natural sources of tryptophan:** Tryptophan, an amino acid that cannot be manufactured in the body but must be obtained from the diet, is the catalyst that jump starts the body's production of serotonin, the neurotransmitter that regulates sleep, appetite, mood, and pain. Until 1989 synthesized tryptophan was sold widely in health-food stores, used by those seeking to improve sleep. In fact, there is evidence to suggest that tryptophan does have a positive effect on inducing sleep: Hauri, in *No More Sleepless Nights*, cites more than two dozen studies showing that 50 percent of all insomnia under study has been helped by tryptophan administration. In 1989, however, the Food and Drug Administration removed tryptophan from the market for further review and currently has plans to allow the supplement back on the market. (Regulated as a nonaddictive sleep aid, it is available in Canada.)

Tryptophan can be obtained from natural sources: milk, poultry, cottage cheese, eggs, halibut, ice cream, lima beans, liver, macaroni, nuts, oatmeal, tuna, turkey, parmesan cheese, peanut butter, and rice. You should know, however, that eating tryptophan-rich foods does not mean the substance will go directly to your brain. Amino acids compete among themselves to get into the brain, and tryptophan often loses. When milk (which is loaded with tryptophan) is drunk, the numerous other amino acids present in milk actually crowd tryptophan out of the brain. We have more to say about milk as a soporific on pages 46–47. (Quoting research on the subject in *Overcoming Insomnia*,* Donald R. Sweeney, M.D., Ph.D., notes that for a therapeutic amount of tryptophan six 8-ounce glasses of milk would be necessary.)

On the other hand, some researchers believe that the best way to boost serotonin production in the brain—and hence, improve sleep—is to eat nontryptophan-containing carbohydrates several hours before bedtime. Carbohydrates release insulin,

*New York: G.P. Putnam's Sons, 1989.

a hormone that reduces all amino acids in the blood *except* tryptophan.

From the particular process of acquiring tryptophan naturally, rather than through supplementation, expect only a mildly sedated effect for an hour or so after you've eaten the tryptophan-containing food and for three hours after eating the nontryptophan-containing carbohydrate.

3
When You Need Outside Help

If you have followed our suggestions to this point, you've seen your family doctor for a comprehensive examination that's ruled out medical causes of your sleeping problem. You've compiled a personal sleep history and two-week sleep log. If you've tried all of the self-help suggestions—and given your body adequate time to adjust—and you're still not getting good sleep, what's next? It's probably time to get professional help from your family doctor.

Your primary physician may recommend sleeping pills, or you yourself may have resorted to over-the-counter (OTC) sleep aids. Surveys show that an estimated 4 to 6 percent of American adults are using prescriptive sleeping pills, while another 3 percent are using OTC sleep aids. Tranquilizers and sleeping pills are the backbone of our booming drug industry.

In 1986, reports Sidney Wolfe, M.D., head of the Public Citizen's Health Research Group, an amalgam of regional surveys showed that 6.3 percent of those 65 and older were using prescriptive sleeping pills, and almost a third of that total had been using them daily for more than a year, even though a majority of these drugs lose effectiveness after four weeks. Although persons 60 and older made up about one-sixth of the population in 1986, they were receiving 51 percent of all sleeping medications prescribed.

Most experts express concern about the misuse of sleeping pills. "Sleeping medications should have only a limited place in contemporary medical practice," said a National Academy of Sciences report in 1979. "It is difficult to justify much of the current prescribing of sleeping medication."

However, sleep research pioneer William C. Dement, M.D., notes that treatment of a transient problem with a short-term course of sleep drugs can help end sleep problems before they become chronic. Dement believes the medical community must improve its understanding of the role of medications in the treatment of insomnia and other sleep problems, learning to better determine when drug treatment is appropriate. "Particularly for ... short-term insomnia, pharmacologic therapy can be a viable option and should not necessarily be viewed as a last resort," he says.

In this chapter, we'll give you an overview of what's currently being prescribed for insomnia and what the over-the-counter sleep-aid options are.

Intervention

More than three-quarters of America's chronic insomnia problems have a psychological basis, and many are curable with the right kind of professional attention, according to *The Concise Guide to the Evaluation and Management of Sleep Disorders.** It's important to be aware of the several principal types of psychotherapy used in treating sleeplessness, which we cover here. We'll also take a look at several alternative therapies that may be able to move you to the next level of stress reduction or relaxation, if that's what's standing in the way of good sleep.

✔ **55** *Try nonmedical psychological counseling for your short-term insomnia.*

If you and your doctor conclude that psychological counseling or behavior-modification therapy is the next step in treating your transient insomnia, ask him or her to recommend or refer you to a qualified non-psychiatric counselor for an 8-to-10-week course of therapy. One such counselor might be a psychologist: a practitioner who has a Ph.D., is trained in behavior therapy, and in most states cannot prescribe medications. *Overcoming Insomnia* author Donald Sweeney, M.D., a practicing psychiatrist who deals with sleep

*Washington, D.C.: American Psychiatric Press, 1990.

disorders, reports that "three out of four insomniacs respond positively to this type of treatment [psychological counseling]." Other practitioners who might help are social workers, psychiatric nurses, and perhaps marriage and family counselors. The key is finding practitioners with experience in dealing with sleep disorders. Aside from your own doctor, psychology departments of local universities are also good sources, as are local mental health agencies, walk-in clinics, and hospitals. The American Psychological Association (750 First St., Washington, DC 20002) maintains a list of credentialed psychologists.

✔ **56** *See a psychiatrist for insomnia related to severe anxiety, depression, or some other mental problem.*

Surveys suggest that 20 percent of chronic insomniacs show signs of depression. If you're in that situation, begin by asking your primary care physician for a referral. Community mental health agencies may also be able to refer you to a psychiatrist with experience in treating sleep disorders. Hospital referral services provide names of psychiatrists, but they're just the names of doctors on staff at the hospital. So be sure to ask for those with a specialty or background in treating sleep problems. Call the American

Board of Medical Specialties (800-776-CERT) to ver-
ify the board certification of any psychiatrist.

The chart on pages 80 and 81 provides an overview of psychotherapeutic counseling used to treat
sleep problems.

✔ 57 Try a medical sleep specialist.

Some medical causes of sleep disorders may require
care by a consulting specialist who deals with your
most obvious insomnia symptom(s). An internist with
a background in breathing disorders or in pulmonary
diseases can treat problems related to snoring or sleep
apnea. And while there is no sleep-disorder subspecialty in neurology, a neurologist can treat sleep problems related to the central nervous system. You may
live in a region of the country where sleep breathing
disorders are treated by ear, nose and throat specialists; even dentists may be involved in the diagnosis
and treatment of such problems.

✔ 58 Contact a qualified sleep disorder center.

Sleep disorder centers are usually the last step in your
discovery process. In fact, many sleep therapists
question spending time and money on a sleep disorder center before you have tried most of the tips we
list to improve your sleep.

Sweeney's checklist for when to visit a sleep disorder center* includes: if you've failed to respond to (short-term) sleep medication; if psychiatric or medical disorders have been specifically ruled out; if you suffer from severe daytime sleepiness with no obvious cause; if you snore; or if you have experienced an unexplained sleep complaint that has persisted for years.

Sometimes affiliated with a hospital and sometimes not, nearly every sleep center deals with the full range of sleep disorders, while a few specialize in a particular kind of sleep problem, such as apnea, breathing-related disorders, or pediatric sleep problems. Sleep disorder centers—or sleep laboratories, as they're sometimes called—use diagnostic tools adept at illuminating causes of insomnia that others may miss.

Your medical doctor will share pertinent medical history and files with the center's doctors, who may include certified somnologists (who, according to the broadest definition, are scientists specializing in the study, diagnosis, and treatment of sleep problems), sleep researchers, cardiologists, neurologists, pulmonologists and other medical specialists, psychiatrists, psychologists, and certified sleep-lab technicians, all of whom should have experience in dealing with sleep disorders.

Excessive daytime sleepiness is the main complaint of people who go to sleep labs. Upon examina-

Overcoming Insomnia. New York: G.P. Putnam's Sons, 1989.

Types of Psychotherapeutic Counseling Used to Treat Insomnia

Sources: Jack Engler, Ph.D., and Daniel Coleman, Ph.D., *The Consumer's Guide to Psychotherapy;* John Feltman, ed., *Prevention's How-To Dictionary of Healing Remedies and Techniques;* Donald R. Sweeney, M.D., Ph.D., *Overcoming Insomnia;* and Martin L. Reite, and Kim Nagel, *The Concise Guide to the Evaluation and Management of Sleep Disorders.*

THERAPEUTIC FORM	OBJECTIVE	HOW IT WORKS	INTENDED RESULT
Psychotherapy for anxiety and personality disorders	Designed to help people resolve and learn to manage the emotional issues causing the mental and physical turmoil at the root of their insomnia. Often used when patient does not or cannot follow other measures likely to relieve insomnia.	A collaborative process between patient and therapist, with patient taking an active role in identifying and learning to resolve emotional conflicts causing sleeplessness. Therapists employ one of several principal orientations, often in combination (see below).	Patient learns to link stress to sleeplessness *and* how to express anger and conflict in appropriate ways to relieve stress, thereby functioning more effectively and eliminating insomnia.

Who provides: Therapists include psychiatrists (medically trained, M.D. degree, and subspecialty in mental-illness specialty); clinical psychologists (academically trained, Ph.D. degree, and subspecialty in clinical or counseling psychology); psychiatric social workers (M.S.W. or D.S.W. degree); nurse clinicians or psychiatric nurses (experience in hospital psychiatric units or other mental health nursing); and marriage and family therapists (more than 25 states license, require minimum two-year master's program oriented to couples and families therapy, plus clinical experience. In other states, credentialing varies widely.).

THERAPEUTIC FORM	OBJECTIVE	HOW IT WORKS	INTENDED RESULT
Supportive Therapy combined with insight-oriented treatment	A combination aimed, with high effectiveness, at transient insomnia cases; *supportive* aspect reassures it is a temporary condition. *Insight orientation* helps patient identify, penetrate root fears and/or the psychiatric cause of sleeplessness.	Patient learns to recognize insomnia causes, express anger, boost self-esteem, and decrease tendency to self-criticism; is educated about sleep.	Patient learns to master stress and to apply this knowledge before insomnia becomes entrenched again as form of negative behavior.

Cognitive-Behavioral Therapy	An effective combination insomnia therapy that holds that all behavior (and perception) is learned and can be unlearned.	Helps patient look at how he or she perceives emotional issues that trigger sleeplessness; helps structure and implement appropriate behavior modification by using various techniques to reinforce new behavior patterns.	Tries to bring about changes in habits and other psychological functioning whereby patient corrects self-defeating thoughts that lead to sleeplessness.
Psychodynamic Therapy combined with supportive therapy	Focuses on the subjective meaning of experience and the use of therapy to explore, illuminate, and transform (literally, "move the mind") the way a patient experiences him- or herself and others.	Explores emotional issues accompanying insomnia; aimed at chronic insomnia patient with heavy denial of insomnia cause and psychological reasons for self-perpetuating the condition.	Gives insight to patient about psychiatric conflicts, feelings; seeks to clarify specific issues; gets patient to interpret his or her own problems as prelude to changing, taking responsibility.
Interpersonal Therapy	Focuses on interpersonal relations as both cause and cure of the anxiety or mild depression that may be creating the insomnia.	Works to improve patient's communications, interactions, relationships. Often takes form of marriage counseling, if marriage problem is thought to be contributing to insomnia.	Incorporates relationships with others as most important factor in personality development and, indirectly, in resolving the issues causing the sleep problem.
Psychotherapy for more serious mental disorders	Goals for treating affective disorders (depression) differ from goals of treating anxiety and personality disorders. However, when treatment is concentrated on underlying condition—physical or psychiatric—insomnia in most cases disappears.	Employs combination of individual supportive therapy and interpersonal approach, generally in combination with medication(s).	Especially with patients suffering from depression, tries to make patient more realistic about self-perception.

tion, 70 percent are diagnosed with either sleep apnea or narcolepsy; the rest are found to have underlying organic disorders—for example, thyroid conditions or diabetes—principally conditions that could not have been detected by a routine physical exam.

How can you check on the credentials of a sleep disorder center? Contact the American Sleep Disorders Association (1610 14th St. N.W., Suite 300, Rochester, MN 55901; 507-287-6006). The association evaluates the competence of practitioners who treat people with sleep disorders and sets standards for sleep disorder centers, of which there are 266 accredited programs today. The group also publishes an annual list of accredited members—M.D.'s and D.O.'s who have an expertise in sleep disorders and sleep medicine and who have passed a comprehensive exam administered by the American Board of Sleep Medicine.

The National Sleep Foundation (1367 Connecticut Ave. N.W., Suite 200, Washington, DC 20036) can also let you know if a clinic or program is accredited. Write (do not telephone) for information.

You may be asked to spend a night in the lab, although the majority of patients are *not* asked to do so. Usually only those people with possible physical factors, such as apnea and narcolepsy, are asked to stay. If this is the case with you, you will receive specific instructions about how to prepare for the session, which typically takes place in a motellike room equipped with various medical measurement devices.

In the morning, you are asked to answer questions about how long it took to fall asleep, how well you slept, and other impressions. (See Appendix B for the overnight sleep lab tests you might expect.) Occasionally, in lieu of an overnight stay at a sleep lab, you may be able to select ambulatory home monitoring. Measurements, much like those taken at the sleep lab, are recorded using electrodes attached to various parts of your body. These electrodes transmit impulses to a small home computer installed in your bedroom for a night.

Drugs

✔ **59** *Learn all you can about over-the-counter (OTC) insomnia drugs.*

All bona fide sleeping pills are psychoactive drugs—drugs that alter the mind—and are dispensed in this country only by a doctor's prescription. That leaves an extremely limited field of nonprescription sleep aids. The active ingredients in most are antihistamines (drugs mainly used to relieve allergies). The principal antihistamines in nonprescription sleep drugs are diphenhydramine hydrochloride (brand names: Benadryl, Compoz, Nytol, Sominex), doxylamine succinate (Unisom), and pyrilamine maleate (Nytol, Sleep-Eze).

While the Food and Drug Administration (FDA)

has ruled these substances safe, few doctors or druggists find them to be effective as sleep inducers. Although these medications have sedative side effects and are regarded as good choices for those who abuse benzodiazepines, the major class of sleeping pill, experts consider them to be only partially effective.

✔ 60 Don't OD on OTC drugs.

Increasing the dose of OTC sleep aids does not increase sleep effects. In fact, increasing the dose increases other side effects, including constipation, urinary retention, dry mouth, blurred near vision, and possible confusion, disorientation, impaired short-term memory, and at times visual and tactile hallucinations.* Bernard Dryer, M.D., author of *Inside Insomnia*, warns those with asthma, glaucoma, or enlarged prostate to avoid these sleep aids, which can exacerbate their medical conditions. And prolonged use of antihistamines builds a tolerance that eventually makes the drug ineffective.

✔ 61 Use prescription sleeping pills with caution.

Sleeping medications are intended to reestablish good sleep, either in association with self-help measures or, if those have not worked, after other causes of in-

U.S. Pharmacist (May 1993).

somnia have been ruled out. These drugs promote sleep by reducing nerve-cell activity within the brain.

Sleeping drugs are called by different names: Those used to relieve temporary anxiety and insomnia are *sedatives*. Sedatives that are prescribed for anxiety are anxiolytics, or *minor tranquilizers*; and sedatives taken to help you sleep are *hypnotics*.

Two major classes of drugs—the benzodiazepines and tricyclic antidepressants—are prescribed most often in the treatment of sleeping problems, but benzodiazepines are by far the most widely used, whether prescribed for hypnotic or anxiolytic (anxiety-relieving) use. (See Appendix C for the benzodiazepines used for sleep-disorder treatment.) Michael Segell, writing in the October 1994 E*squire*, notes that "patients who use [benzodiazepines as sleep aids] sleep only 6 to 8 percent longer than usual, but say they are refreshed. Benzodiazepines work by suppressing the deepest sleep stages (3 and 4) and improving the quality of lighter, stage 2 sleep. And they decrease the number of awakenings during the night and limit your ability to remember any awakenings, which improves your subjective memory of how well you slept." Benzodiazepines are effective for only brief periods of time—about two weeks is recommended, on average—and are intended to treat short-term insomnia caused by severe emotional stress or long-distance travel.

The biggest negative of the benzodiazepines is

their potential for abuse. When the first benzo-diazepines, Valium and Librium, made their debut in the 1960s, the drugs were hailed as the new royal family of hypnotics, recalls Dryer. "But what initially looked safe now shows side effects: rebound insomnia, even for short-term ministrations; rebound anxiety, even as late as six weeks after stopping, that consists of rapid pulse, sweating, nausea, tremor, depression, and convulsions; dependency, often co-dependent with alcohol; and next-day hangover, with some accumulating in the body for days. With benzodiazepines, you may feel drowsy, not just at night, but in the day, and experience learning and memory deficits, as well as diminished eye-hand coordination."*

In fact, one of the most important things you should know about a sleeping pill is how long it stays in your body. Sleep author James Perl, Ph.D., explains: "Duration of action is measured in elimination half-life, the time it takes for the body to eliminate half the drug. If the drug has a half-life of six hours, half would be gone in six hours. Half of the remainder would be gone in another six hours, so that, after 12 hours, three-quarters of the drug would be eliminated from the body."† Within the benzodiazepine family there are fast-acting drugs (Halcion, for example, with a five-hour half-life) for people who need help falling asleep, as well as slower-acting versions (Dalmane,

*Inside Insomnia. New York: Villard Books, 1986.
†Remedy (February/March 1994).

for example, with a half-life of one to two days) for those who have trouble staying asleep. A good rule of thumb: Fast-acting drugs tend to have shorter half-lives.

An important side note: The newer hypnotics and minor tranquilizers generally have fewer side effects and are more efficient for treating a wide range of sleep disorders than the older drugs are, although many old drugs continue to be in limited use. These older drugs include:

• **Barbiturates (Butalan, Butisol, Nembutal):** have lost popularity due to their narrow safety margin; high abuse potential; drug-drug interactions; suppression of delta and REM stages; REM rebound if user quits cold turkey; inability to aid sleep within 14 consecutive days if dose not increased.

• **Meprobamate (Equanil, Miltown, SK-Bamate):** tranquilizers that are ineffective for anxiety treatment after four months. They can cause an unsteady gait, impaired thinking, and memory loss.

• **Chloral hydrate:** mostly used on the old, young, or very ill who can't take hypnotics; can cause gastrointestinal irritation; may lose effectiveness in higher dosages (1-2 grams).

✔ **62** *Consider tricyclic antidepressants for fewer side effects.*

Amitriptyline (brand names: Elavil and Endep), imipramine (Tofranil), and doxepin (Sinequan and Adapin) are tricyclic antidepressants. These mood-elevating drugs are often prescribed to induce sleep for certain kinds of insomnia: notably insomnia related to fibromyalgia, other chronic pain, and nonrestorative sleep. These prescription-only drugs are thought to have fewer side effects than antihistamines (the drugs used in many nonprescription sleep aids), although they can cause dry mouth, constipation, rapid pulse, urinary problems, tremors, and impotence. They need careful monitoring when taken by older persons, as side effects are likely to intensify. Stronger tricyclics, including nortriptyline (Aventyl and Pamelor) and desipramine (Norpramine and Pertofrane), are more commonly prescribed for those with severe depression, of which insomnia is a symptom.

Frankly, experts are split on the use of tricyclics as sleeping pills. Those opposed point to the range of possible side effects, especially in the elderly, and urge insomniacs to seek and treat the causes of their sleeplessness rather than medicating it; those in favor of tricyclic therapy for insomnia generally approve of short-term drug therapy to prevent the patient from becoming a chronic insomniac.

✔ **63 Use sleep drugs on a limited basis, if at all.**

Because they may be addictive, most sleep drugs are intended for a use of "no more than two weeks," says the May 1994 *Consumer Reports on Health*. A two-week regimen may not even include using the pills on a nightly basis.

However, many people are using them far longer. The problem is one of tolerance, which leads to abuse: After taking them for a few weeks, a person builds up tolerance and hence needs progressively larger doses, which cause progressively shallower sleep. If the pills (especially the short-acting ones) are stopped abruptly, a person may get rebound insomnia or withdrawal symptoms of anxiety, aching muscles, and distorted perceptions, indicating physical dependency.

✔ **64 Never mix sedatives and alcohol.**

Mixing alcohol with any kind of sleeping aid is dangerous! Alcohol depresses your central nervous system, slowing down your breathing and your heart rate. The combination of alcohol and another depressant—a sleeping pill of any kind—*can be fatal*. This is especially true in older users and in those who have sleep apnea (who should never be taking sleeping pills anyway because of their breathing condition). Further, alcohol use impairs judgment: Drinking makes it much easier to forget what and how many drugs you have already taken.

✔ 65 Know the new sleep drugs that may have fewer side effects.

Several new sleep drugs have either been approved for the market or are in the clinical-test pipeline. While each is being touted as a sleep solution without side effects, it pays to remember that the kingpins of the benzodiazepines, Valium and Librium, were similarly hailed at their debuts, only to have side effects emerge once they had been in longer-term use than clinical studies had allowed. Here's what's new:

• **Approved:** Zolpidem, marketed as Ambien, a sleep medication approved in May 1993 by the FDA, is an imidazopyridine compound, the first chemically new class of sleeping pill in 30 years, says James Perl, Ph.D. Short-acting, zolpidem is said to cause little or no daytime drowsiness, memory loss, rebound insomnia, or tolerance, and has at most only limited potential for physical dependency, according to early reports. It permits deeper sleep than benzodiazepines but hasn't been around long enough to prove other side effects or a tolerance.

• **In the pipeline:** A new pill derived from the hormone melatonin—the brain chemical produced in response to darkness and released only at night—is being considered a possible major innovation for treating circadian disorders and minimizing jet lag. By giving synthesized melatonin in daytime, the body can be tricked into thinking it's night. Neuroscientist Richard Wurtman, Ph.D., of Harvard, who has led sleep-related melatonin research since the 1960s, has applied for a patent to use melatonin as a sleep disorder drug. While it is available now in health-food stores as an unregulated substance, its purity, dosage, and side effects have yet to be tested clinically on a broad scale. The Wurtman application, meanwhile, has four or five years of clinical trials ahead, reports the August 31, 1994, *Wall Street Journal*.

✔ 66 *Consider a new use for an old drug.*

According to Perl in the February/March 1994 *Remedy*, "Two aspirin (650 mg. total) can reduce awakening in the second half of the night, but doing this more than twice a week diminishes its effect. Aspirin acts to induce sleep and makes sleep shallower, so use advisedly if you have a busy next day." Given its tendency to cause gastrointestinal upsets in some, this is not for people with stomach problems.

Alternative Therapies

✔ **67** *Try alternative therapies or short-term relaxation or physical therapies to overcome sleep-disturbing stress.*

A variety of alternative therapies focus on body movement and pressure points to induce stress-free states that, in turn, are thought to help promote sleep. Self-administered relaxation and exercise therapies, such as t'ai chi, yoga, acupressure, and massage, can help clear the mind and relax the body, too. Three significant alternative therapies (and the practitioners associated with each) that treat sleeplessness are:

• **Chiropractic:** A holistic, drug-free approach to spinal alignment that calls on hydrotherapy, electrical stimulation, ultrasound, massage, nutrition, and exercise. Chiropractors hold the degree of doctor of chiropractic (D.C.) and are licensed in all 50 states. Chiropractors believe that misalignment of the vertebrae interferes with activities of the nervous system. If the spine is correctly realigned through adjustments, they feel, the body will be able to heal itself. In addition to helping relieve tension, chiropractors have also been able to help with various posture problems that contribute to sleeplessness.

• **Acupuncture** is the ancient Chinese healing art that is concerned with attaining perfect harmony and balance of yin and yang—the life forces—and the unimpeded flow of energy between them. Sleeplessness, acupuncturists believe, is a physiological symbol of imbalance. To correct this, an acupuncturist places small needles at specific points, known as meridians, along energy pathways throughout the body in order to redirect the flow of energy and blood. As in the other alternative traditions, acupuncture holds that if the balance is restored to the body, the body will be able to heal itself. Acupuncturists are not licensed in all states. Contact your state health department to find out the licensing laws in your state.

• **Ayurvedic medicine** is a system of holistic medicine that originated in India and is among the oldest of the healing arts—and one receiving major attention in the United States these days, namely under the auspices of best-selling author Deepak Chopra, M.D. Like the Chinese healing arts, ayurvedic medicine seeks to put the body in a perfectly balanced homeostatic state. (In his book *Restful Sleep: The Complete Mind/Body Program for Overcoming Insomnia*, Chopra calls insomnia a symptom of an underlying imbalance, specifically a lack of *dharma*, or purpose in life.) Ayurvedic medicine employs natural procedures, heavy use of herbal ministrations, and also yoga exercises and meditation. While ayurvedic healers are not licensed in any state, you may find an M.D. or D.O. who incorporates these principles into his or her practice.

We hope that, by trying a variety of the suggestions we've made, you find your own, custom-designed program for attaining good sleep. Stay with the ways that seem to work best for you and remember that quality sleep is often a learned skill that comes only after old, poor habits are broken and replaced by healthy approaches.

APPENDIX A

•

Major Adult
Sleep Disorders

EXTRINSIC SLEEP DISORDERS

Poor Sleep Habits (Poor Sleep Hygiene)	*Symptoms:* Difficulty falling or staying asleep. *Treatment:* Improve sleep hygiene by reviewing and developing presleep habits.
Drug-Induced Sleep Disorder (Medication-Induced)	*Symptoms:* Drug tolerance; shallower, fragmented sleep; less REM. *Treatment:* Wean from drug to avoid rebound-insomnia withdrawal symptoms.
Caffeine-Induced Sleep Disorder	*Symptoms:* Increased time to fall asleep; less total and deep sleep; less REM; anxiety. *Treatment:* Gradually decrease daily caffeine intake; eliminate any caffeine after 2 p.m.
Alcohol-Dependent Sleep Disorder	*Symptoms:* Alcohol tolerance; less REM sleep; increased awakenings in second half of night. *Treatment:* Eliminate or decrease alcohol use, especially within 2 hours of bedtime. Short-term withdrawal effects: longer sleep onset; more REM and sleep movements; irritability.

INTRINSIC SLEEP DISORDERS

Transient Insomnia (Situational Insomnia)	***Symptoms:*** Most common insomnia, triggered by a specific stress, excitement, anticipation; longer sleep onset; less total sleep time; lasts up to a few days. Caused by good or bad stress. ***Treatment:*** Review, develop good sleep hygiene; use relaxation techniques; short-term (2 nights) doctor-approved drug therapy.
Short-Term Insomnia (Situational Insomnia)	***Symptoms:*** Longer sleep onset; less total sleep; lasts up to 3 weeks; usually associated with acute or situational stress (death of loved one, serious medical illness, job loss, recovery from surgery). ***Treatment:*** Review, develop good sleep hygiene; use relaxation techniques; short-term (2 nights) doctor-approved drug therapy.
Chronic Insomnia (Long-Term, Learned, or Psychophysiological Insomnia)	***Symptoms:*** Difficulty falling or staying asleep 2+ nights/week for month+ (often years); early wakefulness; awaking unrefreshed; better sleep in unfamiliar surroundings. Often begins with stress period; complaints can be fixed over time or vary with stress. Especially affects light sleepers who become obsessed with sleep loss, and self-perpetuating cycle develops. Sufferers tend to suppress emotions, avoid intense, overly exciting sensations; show tension in headaches, palpitations, cold hands, feet, lower-back pain. ***Treatment:*** Review history to rule out medical, substance abuse, pain, psychiatric causes. Improve sleep hygiene; try sleep-restriction therapy, self-control techniques. Doctor-approved short-term drug therapy may be indicated.

INTRINSIC SLEEP DISORDERS

Obstructive Sleep Apnea Syndrome	*Symptoms:* 30+ partial nighttime arousals when breathing stops 10 or more seconds, caused by enlarged tonsils, adenoids, or fatty tissue in throat blocking airway; heavy snoring; feeling unrefreshed; daytime fatigue; headaches; night sweats; choking; gasping for air; shallow sleep. Can cause high blood pressure, other heart problems. Particularly affects men, elderly, obese. Exacerbated by alcohol, sedative use, which can be life-threatening because they depress central nervous system breathing functions that are already overtaxed. *Treatment:* Lose weight; improve sleep hygiene, especially alcohol, sedative drug avoidance; sleep on side, not back. If problem persists, get sleep-lab diagnosis (machinery to regulate breathing can be prescribed). In serious cases, laser surgery may be recommended.
Snoring (without episodes of apnea)	*Symptoms:* Loud breathing caused by soft-palate vibration as lungs struggle for air during delta and REM sleep. More men than women snore; especially affects obese, and men and women over 60. *Treatment:* Rule out apnea; keep humidity in bedroom to avoid dry, swollen mucous membranes. Improve sleep hygiene, especially alcohol, smoking avoidance; lose weight; sleep on side, not back; check for allergies, crooked nasal septum, or enlarged tonsils; elevate head of bed.
Narcolepsy	*Symptoms:* Irresistible, excessive daytime sleepiness; brief daytime repetitive sleep attacks (driving, eating, standing up) regardless of how much sleep is gotten;

INTRINSIC SLEEP DISORDERS

Narcolepsy (*continued*)	muscle weakness attacks, temporary paralysis (cataplexy) while awake (during high emotions) or on awaking with vivid, frightening hallucinations; REM period begins within 10 minutes of sleep onset, vivid dreaming can begin while still awake. Insomnia, frequent awakenings, depression. Often inherited. *Treatment:* Counseling for depression; improve sleep hygiene; schedule short strategic daytime naps; enlist family support; stimulant drugs to control cataplexy, and possibly tricyclic antidepressant regimen as prescribed by doctor.
Periodic Limb Movement Disorder, Restless Leg Syndrome (Nocturnal Myoclonous, Leg Cramps)	*Symptoms: PLM:* Repeated 5–10–second leg contractions occurring in at least three groups of 30 movements each, lasting minutes; feelings of not sleeping, feeling unrefreshed; signs of "tearing up bed" while asleep, daytime fatigue. **RLS:** Irresistible urge to move legs when sitting or just lying down; crawling feelings relieved by movement; daytime fatigue. Often inherited; also affects pregnant women, middle-aged, elderly, and those with anemia, diabetes, spinal, and circulation problems. *Treatment:* Both treated with low-dose sedatives to promote sleep (does not stop leg movement). Biofeedback to increase foot temperature. Tricyclic antidepressants may aggravate. Avoid caffeine. Take daily iron, calcium, vitamin E.

INTRINSIC SLEEP DISORDERS

ASSOCIATED WITH MENTAL DISORDERS:

Anxiety and Panic Disorders	*Symptoms:* **Anxiety:** Increased sleep onset, decreased sleeping time. **Panic:** Night awakenings with sweating, accelerated heartbeat, rapid breathing, sense of anxiety or fear. *Treatment:* Improve sleep hygiene; relaxation therapy; tricyclic antidepressant prescription.
Mood Disorders (Affective Disorders, including Seasonal Affective Disorder)	*Symptoms:* Depression, energy loss, irresistible sleep urges, fragmented sleep, cravings for carbohydrates, tendency to add weight as daylight hours decrease in late autumn, winter. *Treatment:* Improve sleep hygiene; start light therapy and doctor-approved drug therapy.
Major Depression and Bipolar or Manic Depression	*Symptoms:* **Major:** Decreased total sleep time, faster REM onset, shallower sleep, early-morning awakenings; feelings of despair, hopelessness; low self-esteem; low energy; poor concentration; lowered appetite, sexual desire. **Bipolar:** Increased total sleep time, excessive daytime sleepiness; "blue" feelings; low energy. *Treatment:* Behavioral and drug therapy, supervised by a doctor.

ASSOCIATED WITH MEDICAL DISORDERS:

Sleep-Related Gastroesophageal Reflux (Heartburn)	*Symptoms:* Backup of food, acid into esophagus; can result in chronic inflammation.

INTRINSIC SLEEP DISORDERS

Sleep-Related Gastroesophageal Reflux (Heartburn) (*continued*)	*Treatment:* Improve sleep hygiene, especially alcohol, caffeine avoidance; avoid acidic foods, foods that increase stomach acids; don't sleep right after eating; wear loose clothing; elevate head 6–8 inches when sleeping.

ASSOCIATED WITH MEDICAL DISORDERS:

Chronic Pain	*Symptoms:* Constant or erratic pain from angina, arthritis, abdominal distress, spinal or pinched-nerve conditions, fibrositis syndrome; difficulty falling and staying asleep; less deep sleep; feelings of fatigue, depression. *Treatment:* Improve sleep hygiene; medical attention to lessen, eliminate primary condition, often augmented by tricyclic antidepressant therapy; start relaxation and self-control techniques.
Other Medical or Neurological Conditions Affecting Sleep	*Symptoms:* Difficulty falling and staying asleep; less deep sleep; fatigue, depression; caused by such primary conditions as chronic obstructive pulmonary disease, asthma, bronchitis, menopause, chronic liver or kidney failure, Parkinson's disease, congestive heart failure, cystic fibrosis, ulcer, epilepsy, head injury, hyperthyroidism, hypoglycemia, or various cancers. *Treatment:* Improve sleep hygiene; medical attention to alleviate primary condition; drug, behavioral therapy to improve sleep.

CIRCADIAN SLEEP DISORDERS

Jet Lag Syndrome (Time-Zone Change Syndrome)	*Symptoms:* Temporary condition of normal sleep and refreshed feeling after enough sleep, but with sleep occurring at wrong time, resulting in sleep deficit, impaired performance; caused by crossing one or more time zones in a day. *Treatment:* Adapt schedule before travel; doctor-approved 2-night low-dosage drug therapy at new sleep time; early a.m. bright light exposure.
Shift-Work Sleep Disorder (Night-Shift Worker Disorder)	*Symptoms:* Chronic fatigue, impaired work performance, difficulty falling asleep; shallow, fragmented sleep; job, family stress; emotional and gastrointestinal upset; substance abuse, excessive smoking or caffeine consumption. *Treatment:* Improve sleep hygiene; enlist family support; take naps; adaptation to regular sleep, eating schedules; supervised bright light therapy; encourage workplace modifications to shift-change calendar, direction.
Sleep-Phase Syndromes: Delayed and Advanced	*Symptoms:* **Delayed:** Sleep onset difficulty until late night or very early morning; trouble waking; daytime grogginess; alert feelings late at night; depression. Frequently inherited. More common of two syndromes. *Advanced:* Sleep onset very early in evening (6–8 p.m.), awaking for day from 3–5 a.m. Can result from maintaining odd sleep hours or from an affective disorder. *Treatment:* Follow good sleep hygiene; keep sleep diary; use chronotherapy and bright light therapy to reset clock. Rigid adherence to regular bed-, waking times once healthy pattern is established. For chronic cases, tricyclic antidepressant often prescribed.

PARASOMNIAS

Sleepwalking (Somnam- bulism)	*Symptoms:* Complex movements, including sitting up, walking in first third of night (always in deepest phase of NREM sleep); often inherited; can occur as indication of mild-to-severe psychological disturbance; often follows high stress in one who may hold in extreme anger in dealing with frustration, failure, loss of self-esteem. Lasts 30 minutes or less, sleeper has no memory of it. *Treatment:* Follow good sleep hygiene; take regular naps; find secure, safe place (i.e., ground floor with locked doors, windows) for sleeping; enlist family support. Psycho- therapy, drug therapy.
Night Terrors (Sleep Terrors)	*Symptoms:* Victims awake screaming; increased heart rate, rapid breathing, confusion, agitation for 5–10 minutes after waking from attack; may or may not recall what scared them; greatest incidence during first third of night during delta sleep. Triggered by stress, fatigue, chronic anxiety; can signal overload; considered severe if occurring 4+ times/month (when it could be an anxiety disorder). Men more affected. *Treatment:* Create sense of safety, security; try night light; follow good sleep hygiene and relaxation techniques. If chronic, augment with medically supervised treatment for anxiety disorder.

PARASOMNIAS

Nightmares	*Symptoms:* Awaking from unpleasant, elaborate dream in REM stage of sleep, generally in second half of night; marked by anxiety, lack of confusion, and ability to recall dream or dream fragments. Affects more women than men. Occurs in times of stress; some victims have difficulty dealing with resentments, and nightmare is thought to help extinguish anger, negative emotions. *Treatment:* Behavioral, relaxation therapies for helping to deal with stress, anger.
Teeth-Grinding (Bruxism)	*Symptoms:* Rhythmic jaw movement during sleep, accompanied by increased arm and leg movements; sleeper may not be aware of actions but awakes in morning with sore jaw, headache, and (in time) ground-down teeth. High percentage of adults (21%) affected; triggered by anxiety, stress, guilt feelings. *Treatment:* Behavioral therapy can include hypnosis, biofeedback, other relaxation techniques. Dental retainer is often recommended to preserve teeth.

APPENDIX B

•

Overnight Sleep Lab Tests

Where electrodes attach to the body:

• **Head (2–6 overall):** to measure brain waves created in awake state and during various sleep stages

• **Earlobe:** to locate neutral reference (the one area where there's no muscle tension, eye movement, and so forth)

• **Other earlobe:** to measure blood oxygen saturation level (by shining and reflecting light through earlobe) in order to determine how serious apnea is

• **Eyes (alongside):** to measure eye movements during sleep

• **Chin:** to measure muscle tension and relaxation, important in REM to see if your muscles are paralyzed (as they should be)

• **Nostrils:** to measure temperature and airflow in order to determine whether or not you are moving air.

(Occasionally, a small microphone is placed here to record snoring.)

- **Abdomen and chest:** to measure breathing movements (how much air is actually moved and whether you are trying to breathe but cannot), in order to determine whether you have apnea or another obstruction. (This measurement may also be taken via electrodes placed between ribs.)

- **Legs:** to measure whether legs twitch in sleep

- **Chest or back:** to record heart activity (electrocardiogram, or EKG)

Other measurements:

- You may be videotaped under infrared light through a one-way mirror to determine sleep positions and their effects on your sleep.

What the results measure:

- Sleep latency and duration

- Type, severity, and pattern of sleep pathology (e.g., leg jerks, breathing interruptions)

- Clues about other possible organic causes of insomnia (e.g., arrhythmias)

- Patterns of sleeping and waking

- Length of arousals and time needed to fall back asleep

- Effects of a sleeping position on the sleep pattern

- Relative percentages of time spent in each sleep stage

- Relationship of sleep disturbance to sleep stages

APPENDIX C

•

Benzodiazepines Used for Sleep-Disorder Treatment

LONG-ACTING HALF-LIFE

Name: flurazepam **Brand Name(s):** Dalmane	***Length of Action:*** Half-life is 47–160+ hours, depending on liver condition; drug can remain effective as consistent dose for 28 days. ***Pro:*** Absorbed rapidly; reduces sleep onset to 15–20 minutes; reduces frequency, duration of nighttime arousals; little or no REM suppression at lower doses; even at higher doses REM suppression not followed by REM rebound upon abrupt withdrawal, probably due to slow elimination; total sleep time increases. ***Con:*** Daytime drowsiness; suppresses delta sleep; accumulates over time to create problems with impaired daytime functioning, especially for elderly, who risk falling.

LONG-ACTING HALF-LIFE

Name:
   quazepam
   and
   estazolam
**Brand
Name(s):**
   Doral and
   ProSom

Length of Action: Estazolam takes only 20 minutes to be effective but one of its ingredients metabolizes into same long-acting substance found in flurazepam. Half-life is 8–28 hours. *Quazepam* has 39-hour half-life.
Pro: Fast-acting. *Estazolam* decreases sleep latency and nocturnal awakenings while increasing total sleep time and improving depth and sleep quality. *Quazepam* induces and maintains sleep, without rebound during or after; seems to have low potential for causing daytime impairment. Unclear if it's more effective than flurazepam.
Con: Estazolam has mixed results on whether it's most efficacious for decreasing latency to sleep onset since it is so slow to clear the body.

Name:
   diazepam and
   chlordiazep-
   oxide
**Brand
Name(s):**
   Valium and
   Librium

Length of Action: Half-life of 27–37 hours.
Pro: Anxiolytics to induce sleep; good for those with difficulty staying asleep or early awakenings, but no longer used heavily by doctors to induce sleep. When they were first marketed in the '60s, both offered better side effect free sleep-inducing qualities than their precursor drugs, the barbiturates and meprobamate.
Con: Daytime drowsiness; rebound insomnia, even with short-term course of treatment; rebound anxiety can last up to six weeks after stopping; highly addictive, easy to develop co-dependence with other addictive drugs such as alcohol. Possible dizziness, staggering, headache, irritability, weakness, slurred speech, sweating, urinary incontinence, constipation.

INTERMEDIATE-ACTING HALF-LIFE

Name:
temazepam
Brand Name(s):
Restoril

Length of Action: Intermediate-acting, half-life of 8–38 hours, but can take as long as 20–30 hours in elderly.

Pro: Slower absorption rate than other benzodiazepines makes it good for insomniacs who awake in middle of night; increases total sleep time; decreases frequency and duration of nocturnal awakenings.

Con: Suppresses delta sleep; decreases REM during first half of night, with corresponding increase in second half; accumulation and morning hangover; some residual daytime drowsiness; not good for anyone with trouble getting to sleep, because it can take 1–2 hours to work.

SHORT-ACTING HALF-LIFE

Name:
triazolam
Brand Name(s):
Halcion

Length of Action: Ultra-short to short acting (2–3 hours, 5.5 most of half-life).

Pro: Increases general quality, length of sleep; decreases nocturnal awakenings; quicker onset; REM is delayed but not lessened; helps jet-lagged person reset clock. Less effect on REM than flurazepam, temazepam, and other benzodiazepines; least likely of benzodiazepines to create morning hangover.

Con: Suppresses REM in first half; concern among clinicians about psychomotor impairment, psychological adverse effects, and anterograde amnesia (could be a function of dose and pattern). Experts voted in 1989 to more clearly warn of the amnesia risk on

SHORT-ACTING HALF-LIFE

Name: triazolam Brand Name(s): Halcion (*continued*)	package label. Travelers who have used triazolam as a short-acting hypnotic (perhaps in combination with alcohol) often have experienced amnesia. Other withdrawal effects: anxiety.
Name: lorazepam Brand Name(s): Ativan	*Length of Action:* Half-life of 8–25 hours. *Pro:* Relieves anxiety-related insomnia; fast-acting, good for someone who needs to be alert in the daytime. *Con:* Weakness; staggering; amnesia; worry.

Note: All benzodiazepines are psychoactive drugs, and habit-forming, except for short-term intermittent use. All depress the central nervous system. If taken in high doses or in combination with other depressants such as alcohol, they can be lethal. They should not be taken by anyone who is pregnant, and they can react negatively with other medical conditions, including chronic liver conditions. Abrupt withdrawal from any of the benzodiazepines can create severe side effects, including rebound insomnia (insomnia briefly worsens from when a person started taking the drug) and rebound anxiety (in which a person may experience dizziness, nausea, tremors, muscle cramps, weakness and/or depression).

Sources: Bernard Dryer, M.D., and Ellen S. Kaplan, *Inside Insomnia*; Jack Engler, Ph.D., and Daniel Coleman, M.D., *The Consumer's Guide to Psychotherapy*; H. Winter Griffith, M.D., *Complete Guide to Prescription and Nonprescription Drugs*; Peter Hauri, Ph.D., and Shirley Linde, Ph.D., *No More Sleepless Nights*; and Donald R. Sweeney, M.D., Ph.D., *Overcoming Insomnia*.

GLOSSARY OF
SLEEP-RELATED TERMS

•

Anxiolytic: A sedative or minor tranquilizer used primarily to treat anxiety.

Apnea: The absence of breathing for a brief period. A person with sleep apnea has many episodes of apnea during sleep.

Arousal: The state of changing from a lower consciousness (deep sleep or sleep) to a more alert state (lighter sleep or wakefulness).

Benzodiazepines: The major group of psychoactive sleep-inducing and anxiety-reducing drugs currently on the market. Most sleep aids prescribed for insomnia are from this drug family.

Chronic insomnia: A condition of sleeplessness that has persisted for more than three weeks, usually for months or years, characterized by fragmented sleep, lack of delta (deep) sleep, late onset sleep, or early awakening.

Chronotherapy: The process of resetting the body's internal clocks by delaying or advancing bedtime and waking time.

Circadian rhythm: The biological clock in humans, generally tied to the 24-hour light-dark, day-night cycle.

Cortisol (also called **hydrocortisone**): A hormone that controls metabolism and emotions, while also stimulating the body's recovery from stress. When the body's supply naturally runs short at day's end, this action cues body temperature to fall and the mind to wind down, become less alert, and prepare for sleep.

Delta (deep) sleep: The deepest and most restorative stages of sleep (stages 3 and 4), in which brain waves are slow and long and the body is dreamless.

Depressant: A drug that diminishes activity of the central nervous system. Sleeping pills and alcohol are depressants.

Dopamine: A chemical substance in people and animals that, when levels are high, leads to the production of adrenaline and noradrenaline, adrenal neurotransmitters most active during periods of stress or emergency.

DSWC (Disorders of the Sleep-Wake Cycle, also called **circadian-sleep disturbances**): One of four major classes of sleep disorders, including jet lag, shift-worker sleep disorders, and advanced-phase and delayed-phase insomnias.

Dyssomnia: A disorder involving the amount and timing of sleep; examples are insomnia and excessive daytime sleepiness.

Elimination half-life: The time it takes for the body to eliminate half of a drug dose from the bloodstream.

Endorphins: Body chemicals, made from amino acids, that act on the nervous system to reduce pain and affect feelings of relaxation, pleasure, and well-being.

Epinephrine (also called **adrenaline**): A neurotransmitter that is most active during periods of stress or emergency. It stimulates brain activity, alertness, attentiveness, motivation, and mental energy.

Excessive daytime sleepiness (EDS): Difficulty staying awake, even after apparently adequate sleep.

Fragmented sleep: Sleep characterized by frequent awakenings and/or difficulty in returning to sleep; usually prevents a person from reaching or sustaining the deeper and more restorative stages of sleep.

Homeostatic clock: One of the body's two internal timekeeping mechanisms that govern the sleep-wake cycle; every 28 hours the clock triggers a biorhythmic reset of body systems and chemicals, as they are run down or depleted and need rebuilding and replenishing.

Hypnotic: A sleep-promoting psychoactive drug, such as a benzodiazepine.

Insomnia: Inability to sleep or to remain asleep throughout the night. Transient, or short-term, insomnia lasts several (up to three) weeks or less, while chronic insomnia refers to sleeplessness that persists for more than six weeks, usually for months or years.

Jet lag: Temporary maladjustment of circadian body rhythms experienced when a person crosses one or more time zones in a short period of time; characterized by feelings of exhaustion, light-headedness, irritability, memory impairment, digestive problems, and sleep-wake difficulties.

Learned insomnia: A form of sleeplessness that often begins for a real reason, such as a family or work crisis, but persists long after the crisis has been resolved because the sleeper has become obsessed with being unable to sleep.

Light therapy (also called **phototherapy**): A treatment for insomnia and certain forms of depression in which bright light (2,500 lux, equivalent to daylight at dawn) is introduced for differing lengths of time at particular times of day to influence the person's circadian rhythm to reset itself.

Long sleeper: One who normally needs nine or more hours of sleep a night for optimal body functioning.

Melatonin: The neurotransmitter that induces sleep by helping to control circadian (light-dark) rhythm. Secretions of melatonin are stimulated by darkness.

Microsleep: Short burst—of several seconds' duration—of involuntary sleep experienced by a wakeful person who is so fatigued that sleep becomes irresistible.

Minor tranquilizer: A sedative to calm anxiety, also known as an anxiolytic, often prescribed in short-term dosages to help overcome anxiety-related insomnias.

Narcolepsy: A neurological disorder that causes sudden sleep attacks.

Neurotransmitter: A hormonelike brain chemical that conducts nerve signals among the brain cells.

Norepinephrine (also called **noradrenaline**): A neurotransmitter that is most active during periods of stress or emergency. It stimulates brain activity, alertness, attentiveness, motivation, and mental energy.

NREM (non–rapid eye movement) sleep: All the sleep except for **REM sleep;** includes stages 1, 2, 3, and 4.

Parasomnia: The class of sleep disorder characterized by abnormal behaviors during or associated with sleep (e.g., sleepwalking, bed-wetting, sleep talking, night terrors).

Phase advance: The movement of a period of sleep or wakefulness to a position earlier in the 24-hour sleep-wake cycle.

Phase delay: The opposite of phase advance; the movement to a later sleep time.

Phototherapy: Therapy that involves resetting the sleep-wake clock by exposing patient to bright (2,500 lux) light at certain times to reset the circadian clock (which is sensitive to light-dark cycles).

Psychoactive drug (also called **psychotropic drug**): A mind-altering drug. Tranquilizers, stimulants (including caffeine), hypnotics (sleeping pills), and other depressants such as alcohol, are all psychoactive, acting to alter mood and behavior by either stimulating or depressing the central nervous system.

Rebound insomnia: A period of intense sleeplessness—characterized by an inability to fall asleep or to stay asleep—caused by abrupt withdrawal from certain hypnotic or sedative drugs.

REM rebound: The occurrence of greater-than-normal REM (rapid eye movement) activity (the stage of sleep when dreaming takes place) after a person stops taking a drug that reduces the REM stage.

REM (rapid eye movement) sleep: A period of intense brain activity, often associated with dreams, when body temperature and blood flow increase and voluntary muscles are paralyzed; occurs regularly about every 90 minutes.

Restorative sleep: The two deepest stages of sleep, also called delta sleep, that are thought to be most beneficial to restoring and rebuilding cells.

Restriction therapy: An approach to treating insomnia in which the sleeper logs for two weeks the average time actually slept and uses that time as the maximum time allowed in bed. When sleep doesn't come in that period, the patient is instructed to get up and engage in some calming activity until sleepiness sets in.

Sedative: A depressant medication used to relieve temporary anxiety or insomnia.

Serotonin: The hormone manufactured during deep sleep and believed to be the key neurotransmitter of sleep biology; controls states of consciousness, mood, and sensitivity to pain and is thought to affect body-temperature changes.

Short sleeper: One who normally needs only five or fewer hours of sleep nightly to thrive.

Short-term insomnia (also called **transient insomnia**): Sleeplessness characterized by an inability to fall asleep or stay asleep that is three weeks or less in duration; often prompted by stress or a crisis; responds well to self-help.

Sleep: A state marked by lessened consciousness and reduced metabolism when the body purges itself of cellular waste, replenishes various body chemicals that control life functions, consolidates memory, and rebuilds cells. Sleep normally occurs in four definite, gradual stages.

Sleep-clock disorders: A class of insomnias caused by problems with the sleep-wake cycle characterized by inability to fall asleep or waking too early, often thought to arise from a low supply of sleep-inducing melatonin in the system or poor sleep habits.

Sleep deficit (also called **sleep debt**): The state of chronic fatigue that results from continued loss of adequate sleep or from fragmented sleep over a period of time. Sleep debt accumulates and can eventually negatively affect health and emotional well-being.

Sleep disorders: A breakdown or imperfect functioning of the body's sleep mechanism. More than 100 sleep disorders have been identified, generally classified in several major categories: disorders arising from trouble sleeping and waking; excessive daytime sleepiness; circadian-rhythm malfunctions; abnormal sleep-related behaviors; psychologically or medically related problems.

Sleep hygiene: The regular habits and conditions surrounding sleeping and waking, including presleep routines and sleep environment. Poor sleep hygiene is a leading cause of insomnia.

Sleep latency: The time between lying down in bed and actually falling asleep.

Sleep-state misperception (also called **pseudo-insomnia**): A form of sleep disorder in which the sleeper incorrectly believes he or she has missed all or most of a night's sleep.

Sleep-wake cycle: The daily 24-hour human rhythm of sleeping and waking, governed by two clocklike systems: one to promote sleep, the other to promote arousal.

Somnologist: A specialist in the study, diagnosis, and treatment of sleep disorders.

Transient insomnia (also called **short-term insomnia**): Sleeplessness that has persisted three or fewer weeks and is characterized by slow sleep onset or awaking in the middle of the night with difficulty returning to sleep.

Tricyclic antidepressant: A type of drug prescribed to elevate mood in those with particular psychological problems, some of which may be sleep related. Also prescribed for those suffering insomnia due to chronic pain conditions.

Tryptophan: An amino acid that is a precursor of serotonin, the neurotransmitter that induces sleep-promoting relaxation. Tryptophan occurs naturally in the body as well as in many protein foods.

Zeitgeber: German for *time-giver*, a time cue (such as an alarm clock or a sleep ritual) that imposes benchmarks on sleep-wake times.

INDEX

•

Locators followed by a t indicate tables

123

What is the
SEROTONIN
SOLUTION??

It's a new way to stop bingeing,
feel great, and lose weight.

THE SEROTONIN SOLUTION

Discover how to lose weight and
lower stress by eating the
right kinds of food!

THE SEROTONIN SOLUTION

The secret is the neurotransmitter
serotonin, a naturally occurring
chemical in the brain that
makes us feel good.

*Eating the right foods can increase the
body's production of serotonin.*

THE SEROTONIN SOLUTION

by Dr. Judith Wurtman
and Susan Suffes

Available in bookstores everywhere.
From Fawcett Books.